THAT WAS THEN,
THIS IS NOW.
SPRINGWOOD'S NIGHTMARES
ARE JUST BEGINNING...

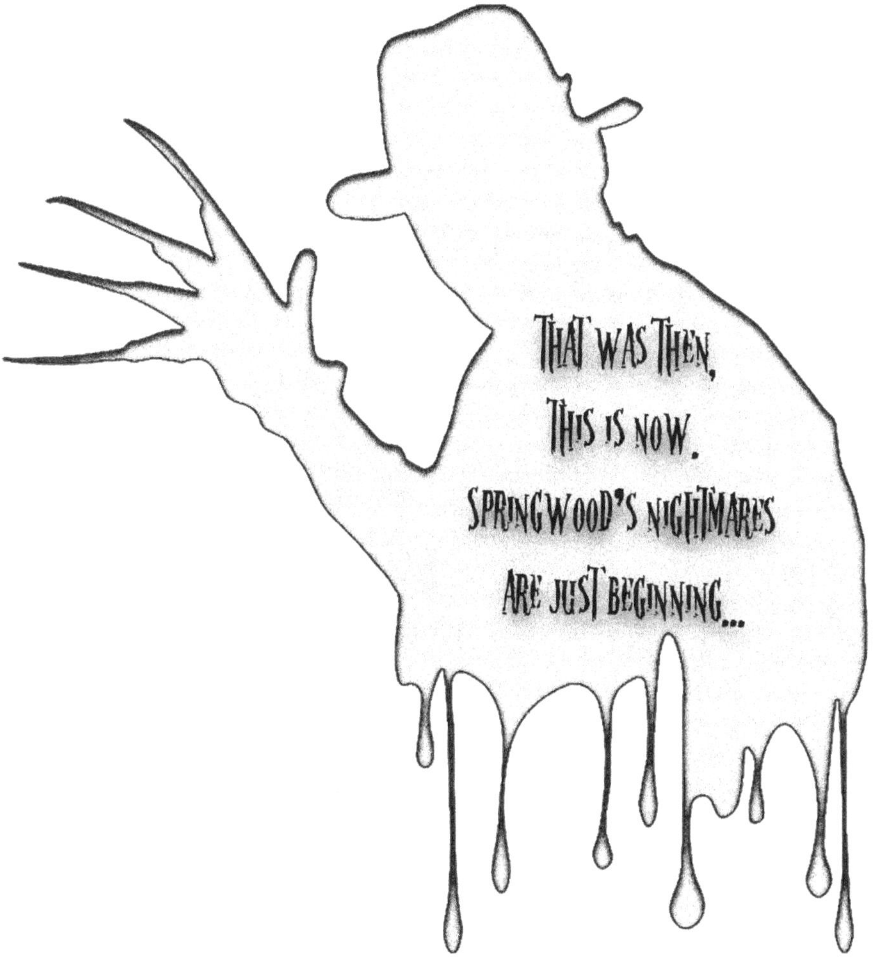

First Edition

Layout and design by Geoff Turner

Published by Death Cult Press
www.deathcultpress.com

www.freddysnightmares.com

WELCOME TO PRIMETIME

THE UNOFFICIAL

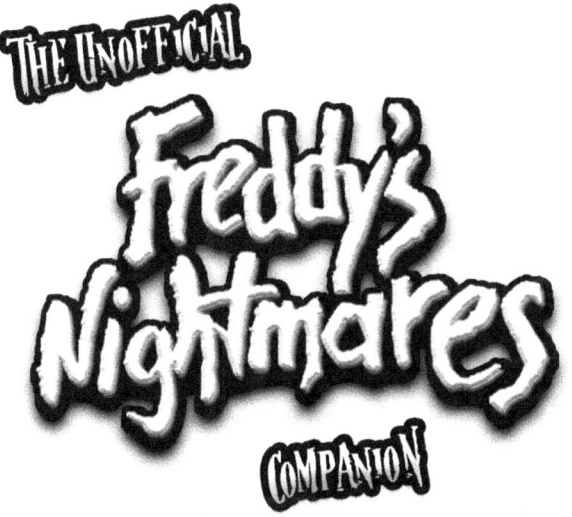

Freddy's Nightmares

COMPANION

GEOFF TURNER

WITH

HENRIQUE COUTO & DAVID DENOYER

DEATH CULT PRESS

DAYTON, OHIO

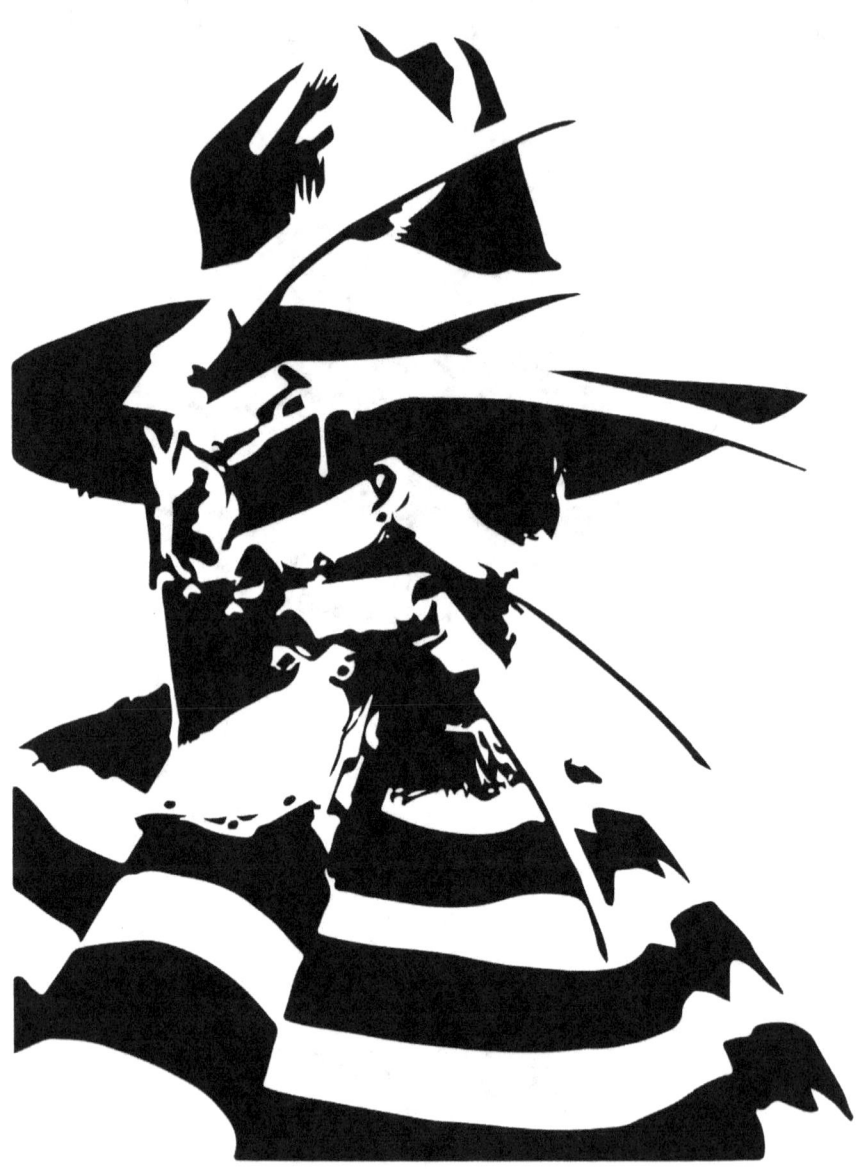

For Ash,
my comrade in arms

This Week's TV Programs

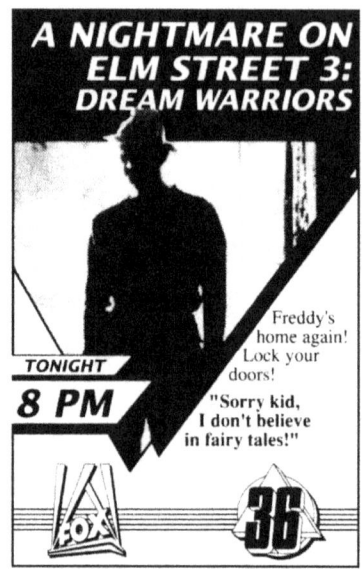

A NIGHTMARE ON ELM STREET 3: DREAM WARRIORS

TONIGHT

8 PM

Freddy's home again! Lock your doors!

"Sorry kid, I don't believe in fairy tales!"

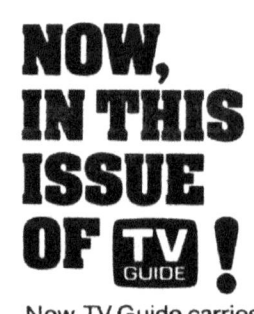
In addition to the listings herein, Chs. 30, 56 and 57 schedule instructional programs throughout the broadcast day. **Cable viewers:** please consult the channel-conversion charts issued by the cable companies to make sure you are tuning to the correct channel number.

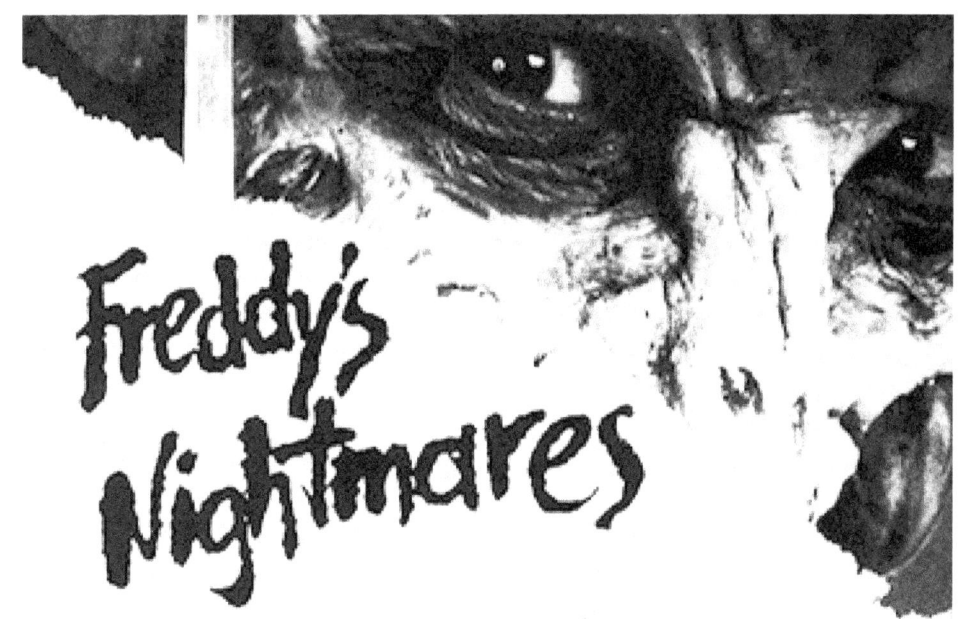

Freddy's Nightmares

Here's a little bedtime treat.

A brand new hour of twisted tales
with Freddy Krueger as your guide.
Venture to destinations unknown,
where the only thing real is the
pounding of your heart.

A **Nightmare**
ON ELM STREET

Freddy's Nightmares
Tonight 10 PM

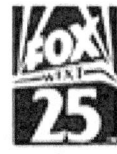

FOX
WEST
25

INTRODUCTION

Freddy's Nightmares was a one-hour syndicated horror anthology television series that aired for two seasons from October 8,1988 until March 12, 1990. In total, forty-four episodes were made, all hosted by lovable child murderer Freddy Krueger, played by genre icon, Robert Englund. The show was created by the newly formed television distribution arm of New Line Cinema, New Line Television and Stone Television and was originally distributed by Lorimar-Telepictures.[1] Based on characters created by Wes Craven, and produced by Jeff Freilich, Robert Shaye, Scott A. Stone and Gilbert Adler, each episode of Freddy's Nightmares takes the viewer back to Springwood, Ohio for new tales of terror from Elm Street.

Each episode of the series features two different short stories, with the second typically structured around a minor character from the previous story. The exceptions to this are the pilot, "No More Mr. Nice Guy," and season one episode seven, "Sister's Keeper," which each featured a single one-hour storyline. Most episodes in season two form small story arcs, where events are referenced in later episodes. Most episodes were heavily edited before their original airings. For example, the season one finale, "Safe Sex," had eight minutes removed.

Freddy's Nightmares has never been officially released on home media, in its entirety, in the United States. Five VHS tapes, containing one episode each, were released domestically on September 11, 1991, by Warner Home Video. Many other countries including Australia, Brazil, Japan, Finland, Italy, Germany, the Netherlands and the United Kingdom released eight VHS tapes, each containing two episodes.

The show was later replayed on networks like Chiller as part of their initial programming in 2007, and more recently on digital streaming services such as Tubi. As of this writing, all episodes from both seasons are available for viewing/download via the Internet Archive at archive.org.

Welcome to Primetime is partially based on the retrospective podcast hosted by Henrique Couto and David Denoyer. Available at www.freddysnightmares.com, *Welcome to Primetime* is sixty-three episodes featuring interviews, retrospectives and exclusive content related to *Freddy's Nightmares*. This companion book includes the aforementioned interviews, a brief history of television syndication, overviews of classic anthology television series and new episode breakdowns based in part on the research conducted by Henrique and David.

In the immortal words of Freddy himself,

"Welcome to Primetime, Bitch!"

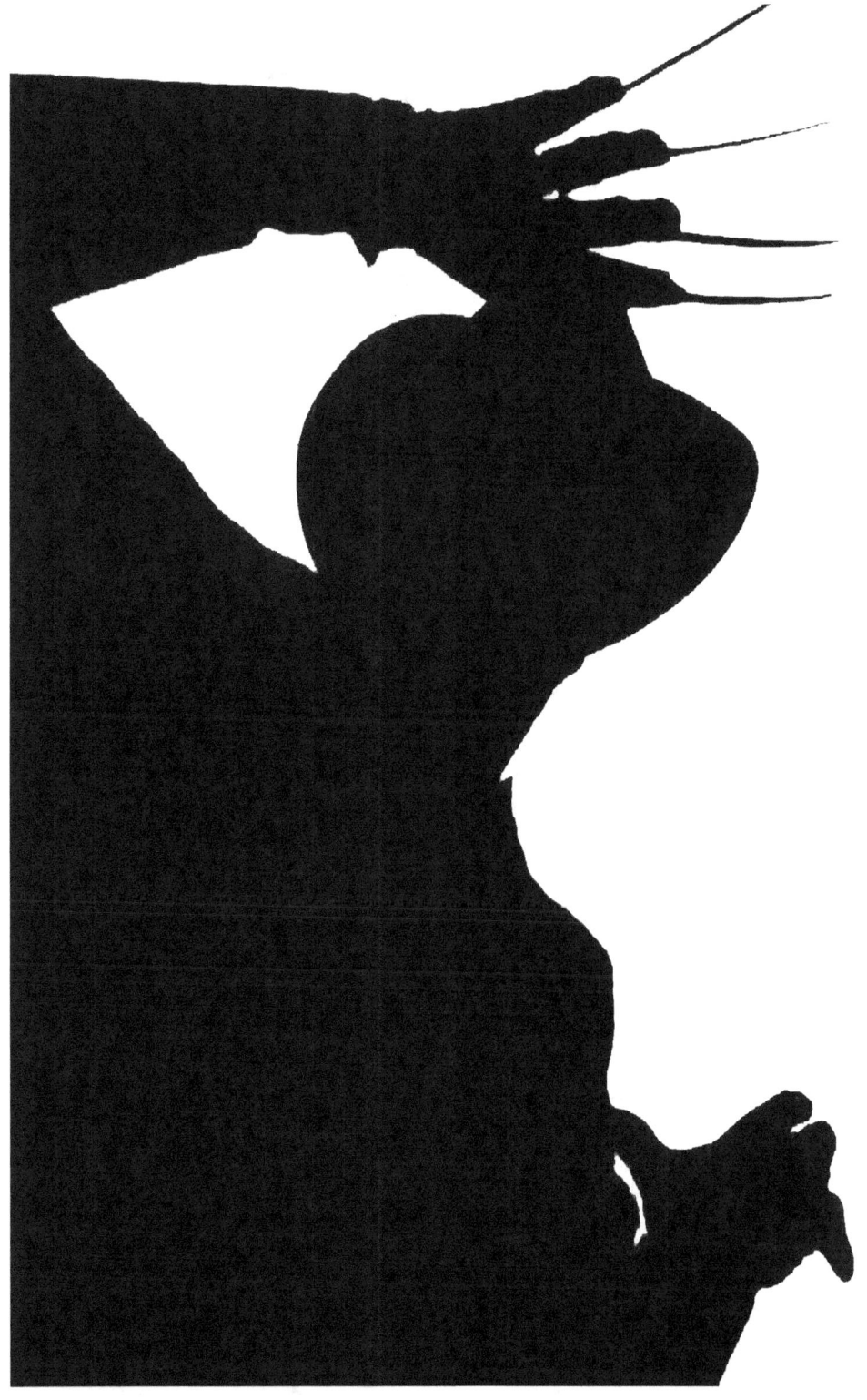

BROADCAST SYNDICATION

THE STRUCTURE OF SYNDICATION

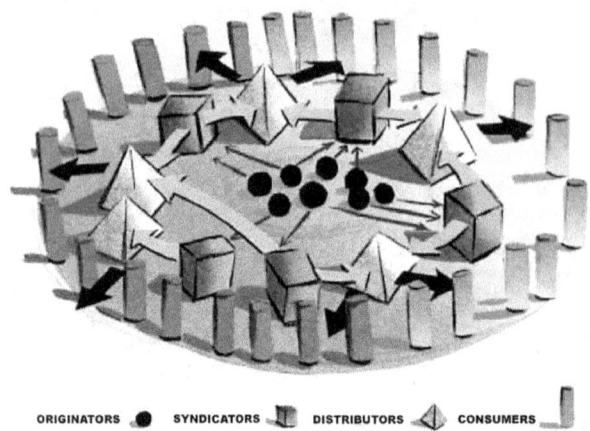

ORIGINATORS ● SYNDICATORS ▮ DISTRIBUTORS ◁ CONSUMERS ▯

Broadcast syndication is the practice of leasing broadcast television rights for a program to multiple television stations without going through a particular broadcast network. Networks generally license a show and run the program on most, or all, network affiliates on the same day and time. When syndicating, a producer or distributor will attempt to lease the show to one station in each market. Syndication is common in the United States due to a lack of centralized networks that are often found in the rest of the world.

There are two types of syndication deals: cash and barter. With cash deals, a distributor will offer a program to the highest bidder. A "cash plus" deal is where the distributor retains some of the advertising slots for their own use. Barter deals are where the distributor would get a fraction of the advertising revenue in exchange for the show. An example of this would be a "7/5 deal," where the distributor would get seven minutes of ad time and the station would retain five minutes.[2] The emergence of barter syndication in the 1980's would cause the number of independent stations to explode from less than 100 in 1980 to over 300 by 1986 because cash was no longer a determining factor for securing broadcasting rights.

The three types of syndication are first-run, off-network and public broadcasting syndication.[3] First-run is where a program is broadcast for the first time as a syndicated show. These types of shows are often made specifically to sell into syndication and are not generally made for a specific network. The most famous syndicated television show is *Star Trek: The Next Generation*. Debuting in 1987 and running for seven years, *TNG's* success would lead to a boom in the first-run syndication market leading to shows such as *Friday the 13th The Series, War of the Worlds* and *Freddy's Nightmares.*

Off-network syndication, colloquially known as "re-runs," is where a show was first aired on network television (or in first-run syndication) and is licensed for broadcast on individual local stations. Shows typically enter off-network syndication when they have accumulated 80-100 episodes or about four seasons.[4] The most common form of off-network syndication is "stripped," this is where the program is played five times a week in the same time slot. In 1988, *Murder She Wrote* was sold in off-network syndication to USA Network for $525,000 per episode.[5] Deals like this could allow syndicated shows to generate profits, even if they had not been profitable during their first run.

Public broadcasting syndication is a parallel service to member stations of PBS. Known today as PBS Plus, the syndication programming service acts as a supplement to the content in the national program service. Some examples of this programming include *This Old House* and *Martha Bakes.*

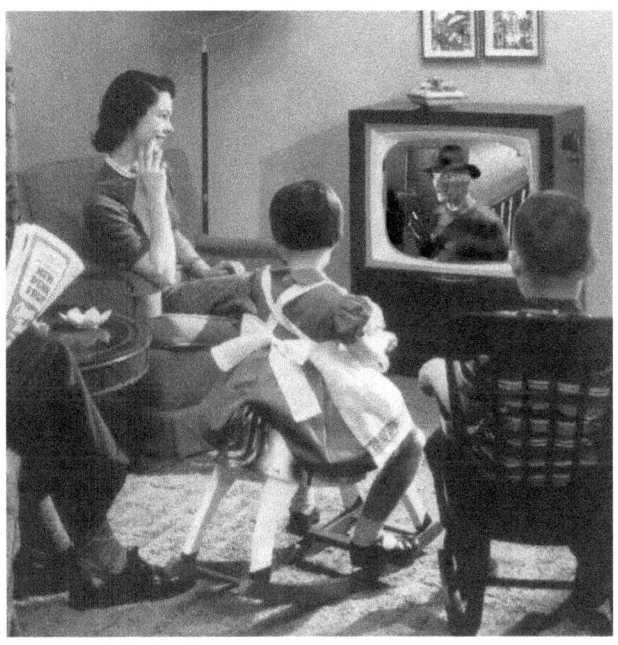

NOTABLE ANTHOLOGY TELEVISION PROGRAMS

Alfred Hitchcock Presents, also known as *Alfred Hitchcock Hour* aired on CBS, and later NBC, from October 2, 1955, until May 10,1965. Three hundred sixty-one episodes were produced in total during the show's ten season run; two hundred sixty-eight as *Alfred Hitchcock Presents* over the first seven seasons and ninety-three as *Alfred Hitchcock Hour* for the last three seasons. The show was created and presented by Alfred Hitchcock, who also directed eighteen of the episodes himself, between the two versions of the program.

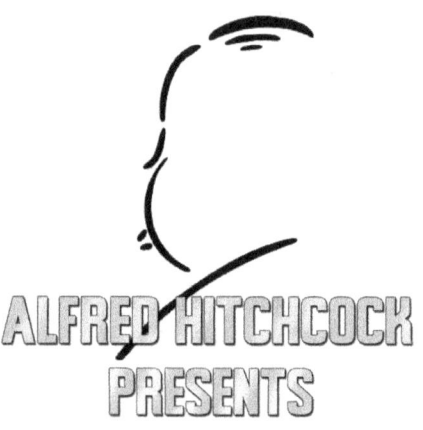

Alfred Hitchcock Presents was well known for the show's intro which featured Hitch's silhouette walking into a sketched outline (drawn by Hitchcock) of his figure with the theme music "Funeral March of a Marionette," by Charles Gounod.[6] This theme music was suggested to Hitchcock by his longtime musical collaborator, composer Bernard Herrmann.

The program has been consistently cited as one of the best television shows of all time and has continued to be popular in syndication in the decades since its original release. One of the most famous episodes was written by Roald Dahl called "Man from the South," starring Steve McQueen and Peter Lorre. This episode was later remade by Quentin Tarantino in the segment "The Man from Hollywood" in the film *Four Rooms*. The series would later be revived by NBC in 1985 with newly colorized footage from the original series.

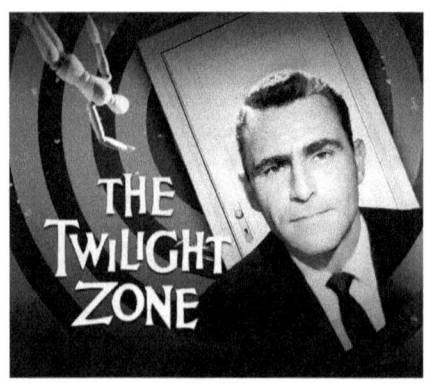

The Twilight Zone was created and presented by Rod Serling and aired on CBS from October 2, 1959, until June 19, 1964. In total, one hundred fifty-six episodes were produced, with Serling himself writing or cowriting ninety-two of those episodes. *The Twilight Zone* aired on Fridays from 10:00-10:30 PM for its first three seasons, with season four moving to Thursdays from 9:00-10:00 PM and season five returning to Fridays from

9:30-10:00 PM.[7] The series was predominantly science fiction, but heavily leaned into the fantasy and horror genres as well.

The show's iconic theme music was composed by Academy Award winning composer, Bernard Herrmann, who is perhaps most famous for his collaborations with Alfred Hitchcock, notably, *Psycho, Vertigo* and *The Birds*, among others. Herrmann's first film score was for Orson Welles' *Citizen Kane*, and his last score was for Martin Scorsese's *Taxi Driver*.

The Twilight Zone is consistently ranked as one of the greatest television shows of all time. The show earned Serling two Emmys and a Golden Globe during its five season run.

Thriller, also known as *Boris Karloff's Thriller* and *Boris Karloff Presents* aired on NBC from September 13, 1960, until April 30, 1962. In total, sixty-seven episodes were produced over the series' two season run. Thriller was created by television and radio producer Hubbell Robinson and produced by his newly formed company, Hubbell Robinson Productions.[8] Robinson was also an executive producer for *Gunsmoke* and *I Love Lucy*.

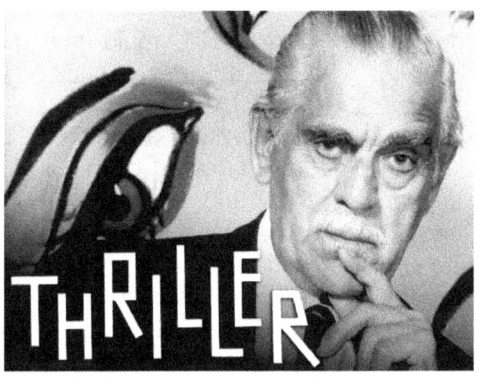

The show was hosted by horror genre icon, Boris Karloff, who would introduce a mix of horror and suspense stories. *Thriller* was notable for its musical score, with each episde of season one featuring its own individual score all composed by Pete Rugolo. Creative changes following the end of the first season led to the replacement of Rugolo with Academy Award winning composer Jerry Goldsmith and his protégé Morton Stevens.

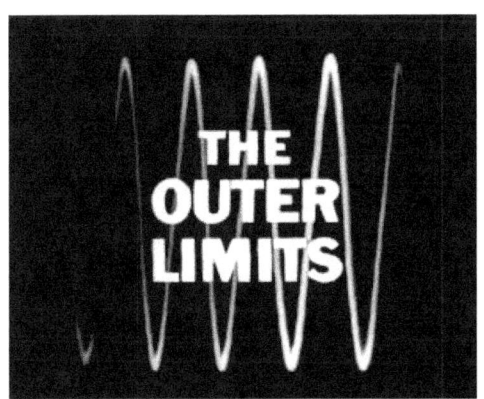

The Outer Limits aired on ABC for two seasons from September 16, 1963, until January 16, 1965, with a total of forty-nine episodes of the show produced. The show was created by producer, writer and director Leslie Stevens and the show's iconic "Control Voice" narration was provided by veteran actor Vic Perrin.

The Outer Limits was more heavily rooted in science fiction than

The Twilight Zone and featured writers such as Joseph Stefano (screenwriter of *Psycho*), Robert Towne (screenwriter of *Chinatown*) and prolific author Harlan Ellison. Ellison is perhaps most famous for the 1967 *Star Trek* episode "The City on the Edge of Forever," which is considered to be the greatest *Star Trek* episode ever. Ellison contended that the inspiration for the James Cameron film *The Terminator* came from his work on *The Outer Limits*. When Cameron conceded to this argument, Ellison was awarded cash and a mention in the film's ending credits.[9]

Special makeup effects were created by John Chambers, notable for his work on the *Planet of the Apes* films and for designing the original Vulcan ears for Leonard Nimoy's Spock character on *Star Trek*. Incidentally, Nimoy had also appeared in two episodes of *The Outer Limits*. Some of Chambers' creatures were later reused in *Star Trek* as well. The show's cinematography is often compared to that of the film noir and German Expressionism genres. Cinematographer Conrad Hill would later go on to win multiple Academy Awards.

Mystery & Imagination was a British television program that aired on ITV from January 29, 1966, until February 23, 1970. In total there were twenty-four episodes in five series (seasons). Series one through four were filmed in black & white, while series five was filmed in color. The episodes featured stories by well known authors such as Robert Louis Stevenson, Bram Stoker, Mary Shelley, M.R. James and Edgar Allen Poe. English actor David Buck starred as the show's central character and narrator, Richard Beckett, in all the show's episodes.

Of the eighteen episodes from the first three series, only two have survived in their entirety: "The Fall of the House of Usher" and "The Open Door." Both of these episodes were part of series one. A brief clip from series three episode, "Casting the Runes," as well as all six episodes from series four and five have also survived. Audio recordings from six of the lost episodes were uploaded to YouTube in 2017. British DVD label, Network, released all eight surviving episodes and the "Casting the Runes" clip on DVD in 2010.

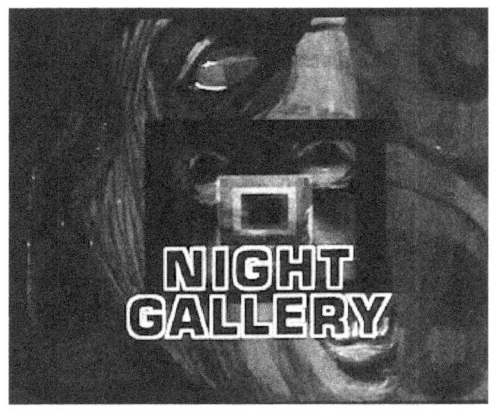

Night Gallery aired on NBC from December 16, 1970, until May 27, 1973, with the show's pilot having been previously aired on November 8, 1969. The pilot episode consisted of three segments, the second of which, "Eyes," was the directorial debut of Steven Spielberg. In total there were forty-three episodes during the show's three season run. Rod Serling created and hosted Night Gallery and served as one of the screenwriters. For Serling, Night Gallery was the logical extension to The Twilight Zone, even though the show tended to be more horror focused as compared to The Twilight Zone's science fiction leanings. The show regularly featured adaptations of classic fantasy horror stories by authors such as H.P. Lovecraft.

Seasons one and two were a sixty-minute format with each episode consisting of an "A" and "B" story. Season three was changed to a thirty-minute format featuring just one storyline per episode. During season two, the show started using comic blackout sketches between the story segments, a change that Serling vehemently opposed.[10] Thirty-nine episodes were severely altered for Night Gallery's syndication package. These episodes were re-edited from their original sixty-minute format to fit a thirty-minute time slot. An additional twenty-five episodes of an unrelated program from 1972 entitled The Sixth Sense were also incorporated into the syndicated release. These episodes included newly filmed introductions featuring Serling and were also heavily edited from their original sixty-minute format to fit the thirty-minute time slot.

Thriller, also known as Menace, was a British television program that originally aired on ITV from April 14, 1973, until May 22, 1976. The show consisted of forty-three episodes across six series. Thriller was created by Brian Clemens, who also served as the show's primary screenwriter. Clemens is perhaps most famous for being the primary screenwriter for the British espionage television series, The Avengers.

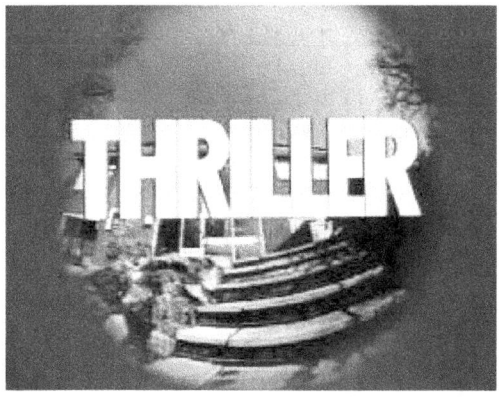

Each episode of Thriller featured its own self-contained storyline and a completely new cast. The only exception to this is the character Matthew Earp, played by British actor Dinsdale Landen, who was featured in two episodes.

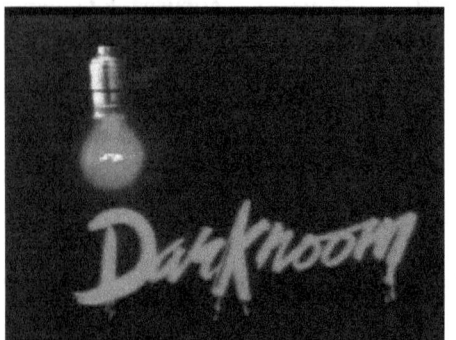

Darkroom was a short-lived anthology series that aired on ABC from November 27, 1981, until July 8, 1982. Seven sixty-minute episodes featuring two or more segments (sixteen segments total) were produced. The segments and episode wraparounds were hosted by veteran Western film actor, James Coburn.

The pilot episode was directed by Rick Rosenthal and Paul Lynch, directors of *Halloween II* and *Prom Night*, respectively.[11] Lynch would direct four segments of the series and Rosenthal would direct three. The show ran in syndication (unusual for a program with so few episodes) on the USA Network in the 1980s and would later rerun on the Sci-Fi Channel.

The *Hitchhiker* was a United States, Canada and France co-production that aired on HBO, and later the USA Network, from November 23, 1983, until February 22, 1991. Six seasons consisting of eighty-five total episodes were produced, with the first four seasons of thirty-nine episodes airing on HBO and the last two seasons of forty-six episodes on the USA Network.

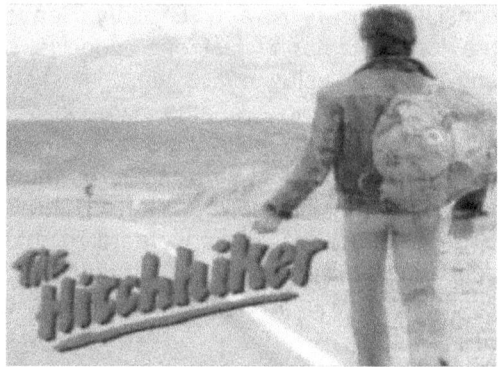

Each episode was introduced and concluded by "The Hitchhiker," played by Nicholas Campbell for the first three episodes and by Page Fletcher for the remaining eighty-two episodes. After 1983, but prior to the show's syndication, the first three episodes were re-edited to feature Page Fletcher as the title character.

Notably, Paul Verhoeven directed the season three episode "Last Scene." The show entered syndication in 1995 with the HBO episodes having to be re-edited for nudity, language, gore and running time.[12]

Tales from the Darkside was a syndicated television program created by George A. Romero and Richard Rubinstein's company Laurel Entertainment. The pilot episode was broadcast on October 29, 1983, and the series was picked up, with season one premiering on September 30, 1984. *Tales from the Darkside* would run for four seasons, ninety-four (two unaired) episodes, until July 24, 1988.

Tribune Broadcasting syndicated the show to individual stations, most of which aired the program after midnight. Laurel Entertainment had originally intended for the series to be based on their moderately successful 1982 film, *Creepshow*. However, Warner Brothers owned some elements of *Creepshow*, leading to Laurel choosing to omit those aspects, which included the framing device and elements based directly on the comic book style of the film.[13]

Tales from the Darkside featured stories or teleplays by notable authors including Harlan Ellison, Clive Barker, Michael McDowell, Robert Bloch and Stephen King. Each episode featured a narration written by George Romero and performed by Paul Sparer. Tom Savini made his directorial debut with episode seven, "Inside the Closet," which aired on November 21, 1984, while Jodie Foster made her directorial debut with season four, episode fifteen, "Do Not Open this Box," which aired on May 15, 1988.

Richard Rubinstein and Laurel Entertainment would go on to create the anthology series Monsters as well as the 1990 film, *Tales from the Darkside: The Movie.*

Amazing Stories was created by Steven Spielberg and his company Amblin Entertainment and aired on NBC from September 29, 1985, until April 10, 1987. Forty-five episodes were produced for the series' two season run. Spielberg directed the show's pilot episode, "Ghost Train." *Amazing Stories* featured the work of many notable directors including Peter Hyams, Burt Reynolds, Clint East- 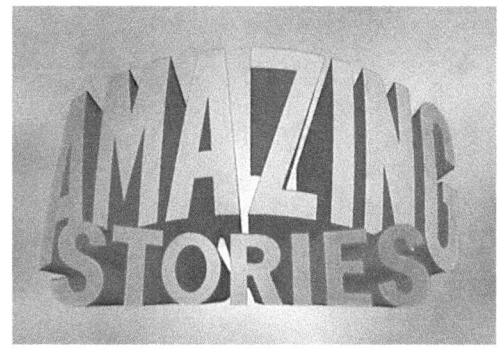 wood, Bob Clark, Joe Dante, Martin Scorsese, Irvin Kershner, Danny DeVito, Tom Holland, Mick Garris, Robert Zemeckis and Tobe Hooper.

The 1987 film, *Batteries not Included*, was originally planned to be a segment for an episode of *Amazing Stories*, but Spielberg felt that the story would work better as a feature.[14] Several episodes were re-edited into six TV movies in 1992.

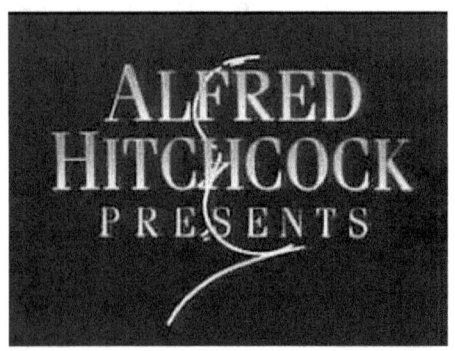

In 1985, NBC aired a made for TV movie based upon the original 1955 series, *Alfred Hitchcock Presents*, using newly colorized footage of Hitchcock. The film was a ratings success and was subsequently ordered to series. The rebooted series, also titled *Alfred Hitchcock Presents*, aired from September 29, 1985, until July 22, 1989.

Four seasons in total were produced with seventy-six episodes; with the show first airing on NBC, who would cancel the series after the first season, and was then revived by the USA Network for the remaining three seasons. The program was once again hosted by Alfred Hitchcock, using colorized footage from the original series. Famously, Tim Burton directed the season one episode, "The Jar," which aired on April 6, 1986.

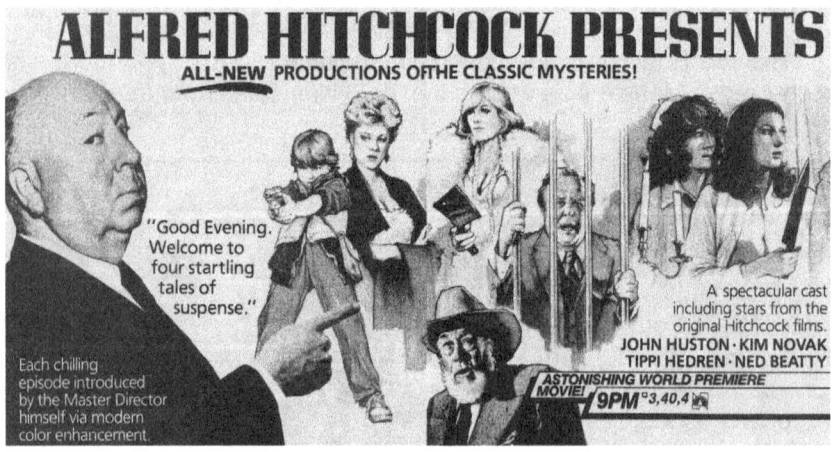

Rod Serling sold CBS the rights to *The Twilight Zone* after the original series ended in 1964.[15] In 1983 Warner Brothers would revive the property in the Steven Spielberg produced film, *The Twilight Zone: The Movie*. While reviews of the film were mixed, there was enough interest generated to convince CBS to reboot the series in late 1985.

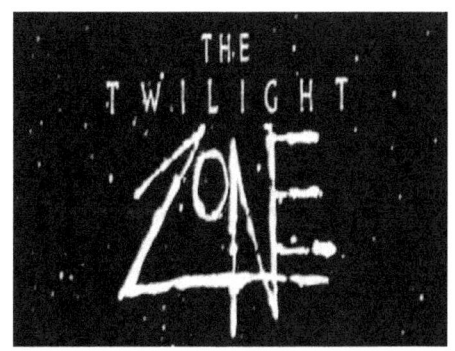

The Twilight Zone would air on CBS and syndication from September 27, 1985, until April 15, 1989. Three seasons were produced, two for CBS and one exclusively for syndication, with a total of sixty-five episodes. The show featured an opening theme performed by The Grateful Dead. Notable writers included Harlan Ellison and George R.R. Martin, while some of the notable directors would include Wes Craven and William Friedkin.

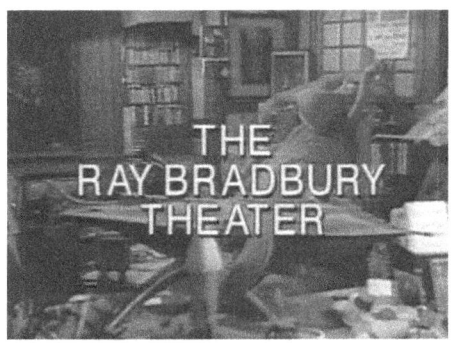

The Ray Bradbury Theater aired from May 21, 1985, until October 30, 1992. Season one was broadcast on HBO and seasons two through six were broadcast on the USA Network. Sixty-five episodes were produced for the series, with all episodes written by Ray Bradbury, based on his short stories and novels. Bradbury would also occasionally appear on-screen to introduce the stories.

Monsters was a syndicated television program produced by Richard Rubinstein and Laurel Entertainment. The series aired from October 22, 1988, until April 1, 1991, with a total of seventy-two episodes across three seasons. The idea for *Monsters* grew out of Laurel's previous effort, *Tales from the Darkside*.[16]

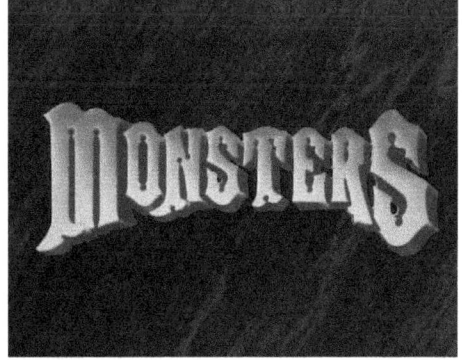

The initial production of the series was delayed due to the writer's strike of 1988, with production officially beginning August 8, 1988, the day after the strike ended, and only seventy-five days before the show premiered.[17] Episodes had a budget of roughly $200,000 would each feature a different monster who would be central to that episode's storyline.

The show's pilot episode was directed by Michael Gornick, perhaps best known as the cinematographer for George Romero on the films *Martin, Dawn of the Dead, Creepshow, Knightriders* and *Day of the Dead*. Gornick also directed the *Creepshow* sequel, *Creepshow 2*. Special makeup effects artists Mark Shostrom and Greg Cannom also directed episodes. Oscar winning special makeup effects artist Dick Smith served as a makeup consultant for the series.

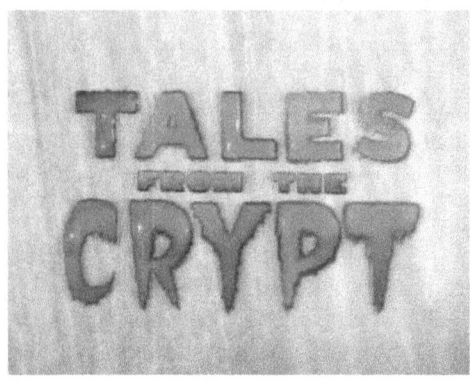

Tales from the Crypt aired on HBO from June 10, 1989, until July 19, 1996. Ninety-three episodes were produced for the show's seven season run. *Tales from the Crypt* was produced by Richard Donner, David Giler, Walter Hill, Joel Silver and Robert Zemeckis. Episodes were primarily based on the EC Comics properties including *Tales from the Crypt, The Vault of Horror* and *The Haunt of Fear*. The show was hosted by the Cryptkeeper, a reanimated corpse, an animatronic puppet which was created by special effects maestro Kevin Yagher and was voiced by the inimitable John Kassir.

The series was spun off into a cartoon called *Tales from the Cryptkeeper,* and several films including *Tales from the Crypt Presents: Demon Knight* and *Tales from the Crypt Presents: Bordello of Blood*. The show contained scenes of graphic violence, profanity, sex and nudity, a perk of being on the premium cable service HBO.

Tales from the Crypt featured episodes directed by many famous and notable directors. Walter Hill, Richard Donner, Robert Zemeckis, Tom Holland, Mary Lambert, Arnold Schwarzenegger, Chris Walas, Fred Dekker, Jack Sholder, Kevin Yagher, Michael J. Fox, Tobe Hooper, Tom Hanks, William Friedkin, Peter Medak, John Frankenheimer, Kyle MacLachlan, Russell Mulcahy, William Malone, Mick Garris and Freddie Francis (director of the 1972 film version of *Tales from the Crypt*) to name just a few. Many of the crew and producers from *Freddy's Nightmares* moved on to *Tales from the Crypt* when *Nightmares* ended its run.

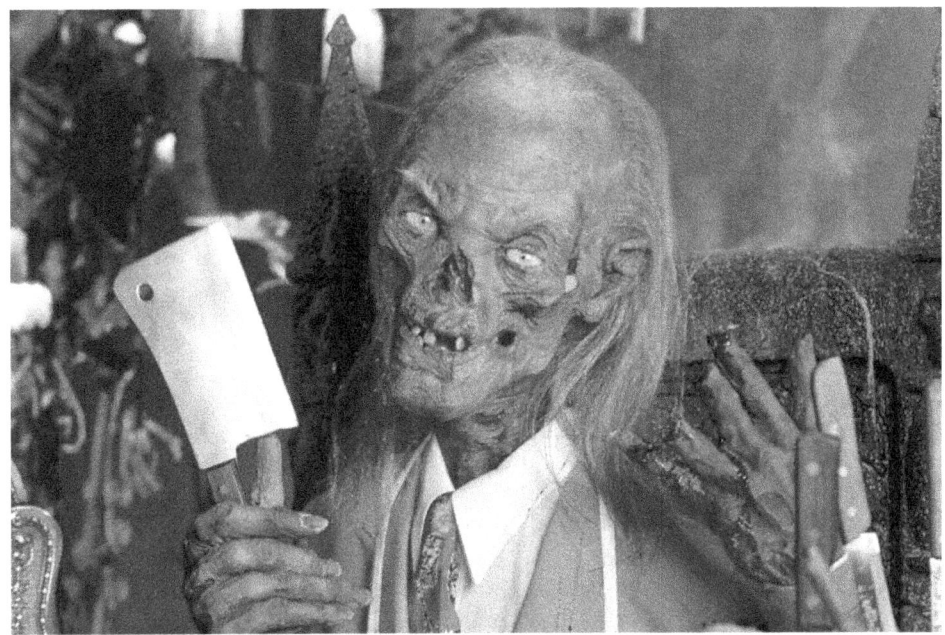

The Pilot episode of *Are You Afraid of the Dark?* aired first on YTV in Canada on October 31, 1990, and then nearly a year later, on October 25, 1991, on Nickelodeon in the United States. The series was picked up by Nickelodeon and would premiere on their Saturday night block, *SNICK*, on August 15, 1992, and would run until April 20, 1996. The series would later be revived from 1999-2000 and again from 2019-2022. The original run was sixty-five episodes over five 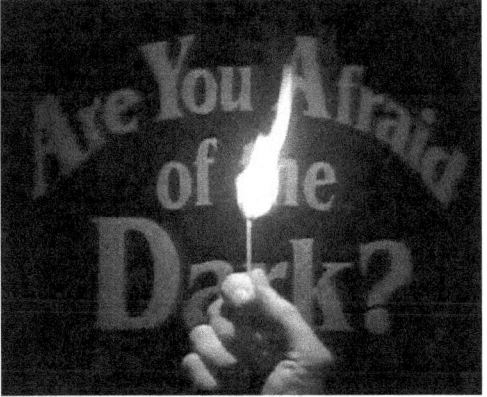 seasons, but in total there have been ten seasons with one hundred and four episodes. Many of the show's stories were based on public domain fairy tales and urban legends. Episodes were introduced by The Midnight Society, a group of youths who would gather around a campfire to tell scary stories. The bulk of the original series was directed by D.J. MacHale, Ron Oliver and David Winning.

NEW LINE CINEMA
NEW LINE TELEVISION

Robert Shaye founded New Line Cinema in his New York apartment in 1967 with a $1,000 initial investment. Shaye had earned his bachelor's degree in business from the University of Michigan and would go on to earn a law degree from Columbia University before traveling abroad to Sweden on a scholarship to study copyright law.[18] New Line made a name for itself distributing public domain films like *Reefer Madness* to college campuses in the late 60s and early 70s. John Waters' *Pink Flamingos* was wildly successful for New Line in both the college campus environment as well as midnight shows in theaters in major cities around the country. In

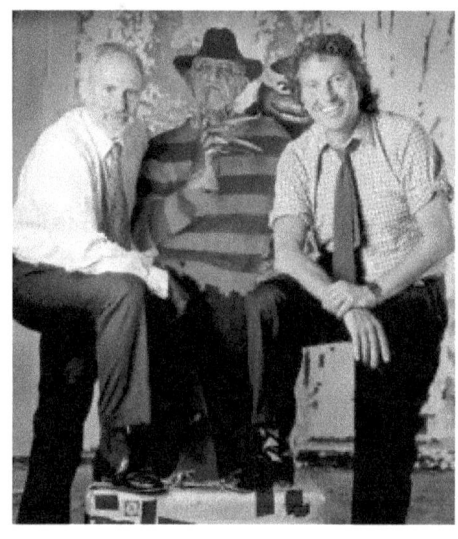

1978 New Line Cinema would distribute a 16mm re-release of *Night of the Living Dead*, primarily on the college campus circuit.

The company entered into the production side of the business with the 1977 film *Stunts*, directed by Mark L. Lester. New Line would expand the production business in the 1980s with films like *Alone in the Dark* and *Polyester*. *Polyester's* marketing would include a new riff on an old theatrical gimmick called "Smell-O-Vision," renamed as "Odorama," where audience members were provided with scratch and sniff cards to be utilized at specific points during the movie.[19] 1984 would bring the studio's greatest success to date, when they produced and released the Wes Craven film, *A Nightmare on Elm Street*. The success of the eventual franchise would lead the studio to be nicknamed "The House that Freddy Built."[20]

New Line Television was the TV production arm of New Line Cinema and was active for 20 years from 1988 until 2008. The division was originally founded by Robert Shaye to produce *Freddy's Nightmares*, but went on to produce other shows primarily based on New Line film properties.[21] These shows were mostly animated programming and included titles such as: *The Mask: Animated Series, Dumb & Dumber, Mortal Kombat: Defenders of the Realm, Mortal Kombat: Conquest, Blade: The Series* and *Friday: The Animated Series*. New Line Television also produced several reality TV series as well as the 2002-2003 revival of *The Twilight Zone*.

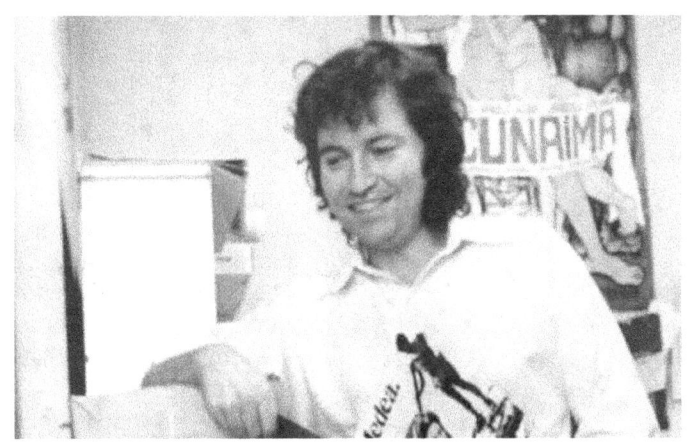

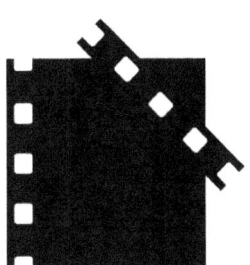

NEW LINE TELEVISION

GILBERT ADLER

ALAN KATZ

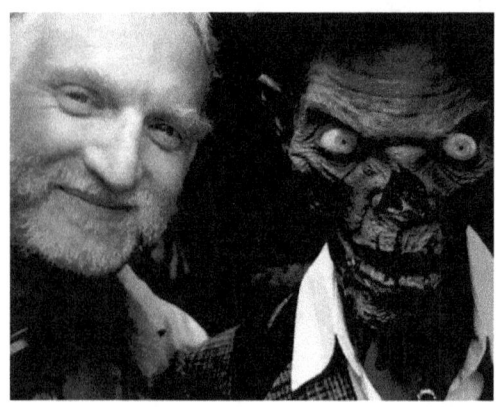

Gilbert Adler is an American film producer who began his career by producing Brian DePalma's 1979 film *Home Movies*. After moderate success in the early 1980s, Adler would branch out into television, producing both seasons of *Freddy's Nightmares,* also writing four episodes and directing one. Alder would go on to find much success producing HBO's *Tales from the Crypt*. He produced two *Tales from the Crypt* spin off movies: *Tales from the Crypt Presents: Demon Knight* and *Tales From the Crypt Presents: Bordello of Blood* the latter of which he also co-wrote and directed.

In 1999 Adler formed Dark Castle Entertainment with Joel Silver and Robert Zemeckis. Dark Castle is notable for producing *House on Haunted Hill* (1999), *Thirteen Ghosts* (2001), *Ghost Ship* (2002) and others. Adler was also a producer on the 2004 film version of *Starsky and Hutch, Constantine* (2005), *Superman Returns* (2006) and *Valkyrie* (2008).

Alan L. Katz is an American film and television producer, writer and script editor. Katz got his start in television writing four episodes for *Freddy's Nightmares*, "Freddy's Tricks and Treats," "Welcome to Springwood," "Bloodlines" and "Funhouse." Katz is perhaps most famous for his work on the HBO series *Tales from the Crypt* for which he served as a story editor, screenwriter and later co-producer for the series beginning on the show's third season.

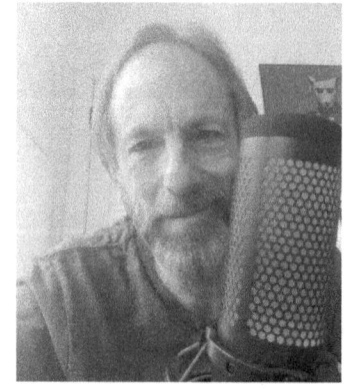

In 1992 Katz wrote the screenplay for

24

Children of the Corn II: The Final Sacrifice before returning to the *Tales from the Crypt* franchise by co-writing the screenplay for *Tales From the Crypt Presents: Bordello of Blood* with Gil Adler in 1996. Katz has also made cameo appearances in episodes of *Freddy's Nightmares* and *Tales from the Crypt* that he also wrote, "The Funhouse," and "Whirlpool," respectively.

Interview conducted by
Henrique Couto and David Denoyer

HC: What were you working on prior to coming onboard *Freddy's Nightmares*?

AK: I had a couple screenplays in development and that was pretty much it. I had no TV experience before that show. The thing that really worked for me was being partnered with Gil. Gil was one of the first people that I met when I came to Los Angeles in 1985. I grew up in Baltimore, went to school in New York, I was a drama major at Vassar. At this point I was living in New York, I thought I was going to go into the theater so I was just writing plays. To me, Los Angeles was the stupidest place in the whole world. It was the land of the avocado head. I had a friend from high school, Carol Yumkas, she had become an agent for William Morris in Los Angeles and she said to me, "You should try writing a screenplay," and I had been toying with the idea, so I wrote one. She said, "This is pretty good, you should come out to meet and greet people," and I thought, OK, what have I got to lose, stupid place, I'll go there and I'll come back.

It was June 1985, Los Angeles was very different then, it was a lot less crowded, a lot less traffic, but it was really pretty. I grew up in the East and in June its warm and humid, in New York, the city already smells, you walk around and it smells like piss half the place. Los Angeles is the desert, it's dry, there is no humidity, the weather was fantastic. The people were just so nice to me, I had written this script and everyone liked it. One day Carol took me to a Hollywood premiere, *St. Elmo's Fire,* and that was incredibly intoxicating, to rub elbows and share canapé trays with all those people. My fourth day in Los Angeles, I didn't have any meetings and someone suggested that I take a drive through Topanga Canyon and by the time I had gotten to the Pacific Coast Highway, where the mountains literally plunge into the ocean, I was done, I had given up on the East Coast. I completely sold my soul and the very next month I moved out to the land of the avocado head. Something about this place and this business just appealed to me.

One of the first producers that I had met that week was Gil and he liked the script I had written and wanted to hear what else I was pitching. He liked what I was pitching so he found some money and the next thing you know, we were working on a screenplay together. We found that we really liked the process of writing together, it was very natural and it was just great fun to do. Gil had trained as an accountant, he worked in the office of a guy named Sid Finger who did the books on all the James Bond pictures. So Gil's understanding is an accountants understanding and as a producer, if you have $1.00 to spend, don't spend $1.01, you don't have it, but if you can do it for $0.99, thats even better, provided that the quality is the same as for $1.00. It's no good saying no to solving a problem, part of how you do it is that you get really creative with the storytelling, and that starts with the script. If you are a writer/ producer then you always have control of the means. The wonderful thing about television versus the feature film world is that TV is all writer produced, so the writer/ producer is the power. In TV, a director is just a traffic cop. Being a producer is constant creative problem solving. It is taking everything that you know and applying it to the problem that's coming at you like a freight train.

HC: Was it fair to say that you had a hand in every episode of *Freddy's Nightmares*?

AK: I had my name on a few episodes, but that was about it. I was just Gil's writing partner at that particular point on the second season when Gil directed his episode. That was a fascinating learning experience for both of us because we really had no idea what we were doing. When I look back now at some of the conversations that we had in Gil's office, we were scared out of our minds.

This was huge for us and its not like we were filled with the knowledge that we have now. Gil still approaches directing with a certain amount of, "This is the best approach to it," but with the confidence of having done it a bunch of times now. At the end of the day, most directing is pretty basic: master, coverage, master, coverage. If you do that then it might not be the most visually interesting show, but you'll tell a story. Back then we had almost no concept of master, coverage.

Ironically, by the time we got *Tales from the Crypt*, Gil and I, Gil especially, had become the school for directors. The executive producers on *Tales from the Crypt* used those director slots for a lot of first time directors (mainly the actors who did it). They would have first time potential feature film directors do an episode as a bit of a shake out to see what they knew, and really especially for Gil to train them. So I'm happy to say that there was actual progress between *Freddy's Nightmares* and *Tales from the Crypt.*

HC: Lets talk a little more about when you guys took over *Tales from the Crypt*, the show was on the verge of being canceled at that point.

AK: *Tales from the Crypt* changed television. When *Tales from the Crypt* happened, film was one place, television was another, and you did not travel back and forth between them. Occasionally a Tom Hanks or a Robin Williams would go from TV to film, but you didn't dare go the other way. If you were in film and went to TV that meant that your career was in decline. Suddenly, HBO had TV shows and movie executives approached them and said, "We want to do a new movie every week based on this old anthology comic book series, *Tales from the Crypt*." So when the executives made the deal for *Tales from the Crypt*, they didn't make it like a TV deal where you get a deficit partner, that was all old fashioned to them. So they ended up without enough money to cover production and HBO began covering all of the overages. The night before the wrap party, HBO handed the executives a financial statement that said, "Hey guys, you're a million dollars cash in the hole. Get out your checkbooks." The executives literally had to write checks to cover the overages. So the first thing the executives did was cancel the wrap party and then they fired everyone. They were still contractually obligated to one more season and the partners were going to hold them to that. The executives had to find new producers and HBO trusted Gil because he had worked on *The Hitchhiker* for them.

The original intention when Gil and I came aboard *Tales from the Crypt* was that we were going to see it out, we were going to be its pallbearers. Instead, we turned it around. Not only did we revive the franchise, we took it back to its roots. I was a huge fan of the EC comic books and Bill Gaines' world and to me this was an opportunity to reinvest in that sense of wicked fun of the EC Comics.

At the time, the Cryptkeeper was just OK, he was a funny, mean-spirited puppet. My question to Joel Silver was, "What does the Cryptkeeper do at the end of the day when he punches the clock and stops being the Cryptkeeper?" I wanted to create an internal life for the Cryptkeeper. With *Freddy's Nightmares,* Freddy Krueger already had this great backstory. By the end of the first season, the Cryptkeeper had spent all that a character with no backstory had to spend. To me, it was essential to know who the Cryptkeeper was. That, more than anything, didn't only revive the franchise, it created a franchise, and because of that HBO didn't cancel the show.

We ended up taking that million dollar deficit out of our budget and we actually wound up producing season three for two million dollars less than they had for season two. They weren't producing it like a television show. In the old days, when it was the old paradigm, it was like an assembly line. That's how they did *Freddy's Nightmares.* In fact, the way that we did *Tales from the Crypt*, Gil sort of invented how to do that on *Freddy's Nightmares.*

HC: How did you guys end up working on *Freddy's Nightmares*?

GA: I got off on the wrong stop on the subway. No, no, I knew Bob Shaye from New York when he first started New Line Cinema. He was a good friend of my producing partner that I did Broadway and off-Broadway with, a guy named Jack Temchin. Because of Jack, I got to know Bob very well. Bob went on to have a very successful run with the *Nightmare on Elm Street* movies and they were talking about making it into a series. He called me one day and said, "I need you to do this." That's sort of how it started. He started telling me the specifics of it. The budget for the show was under a half-million dollars per one-hour episode and we had to shoot the one-hour show in five days. I guess I was too stupid to say no, so I said, "Sure, no problem."

Well, we get to doing the show and we actually had to pull it off. That was up to us to figure out. How do you shoot the hour in five days, which means you're shooting ten pages a day, every day, and there are no days off for writing. On the sixth day, you start episode two, and you do twenty-two of them. Initially, they wanted twenty-two hours and they said, "You know, foreign [sales] we want to be able to distribute them as motion pictures, so we'd like you guys to write them so they work as one hours, but they also work if you put two of them together to make a movie." The first season, that was the mandate. For the second season they came in and said, "We want them as half-hours, and hours, and two-hours."

AK: Did it ever released this way? I'm sure not. It was just a masturbatory exercise.

GA: We would have to write them and conceive of them with all that in mind. The two of us in my house and his house working on this would be like, "What are we matching this with to make the two-hour?" It was just crazy, and really we were the only two guys to talk to each other to figure it out. There wasn't a staff of writers, we would have some people come in, but ultimately it all went through Alan's typewriter. We would look at it and say, " How are we gonna do this? How are we gonna do that? How does this work in five days? How can we shoot it?" It was kind of mind boggling and when you think about it now, all those years ago, doing ten pages a day every day, anyone who came in to direct did ten pages a day.

AK: The hardest part of the challenge was the first six episodes. The show started during the 1988 writer's strike and because of that, they couldn't hire guild writers. At that point I wasn't in the writer's guild. I remember there was a meeting in a hotel room at the Chateau Marmont, Bob Shaye had a bunch of the writers there, Gil and I were there as well, and they explained the deal to us. They were going to pay $6,000 for each script. Bob Shaye said, "Here's what we think it's kinda gonna be…" At this point they would have had us write all twenty-two episodes if the strike hadn't ended. But after we had written six episodes, the strike ended and they went and hired Jonathan Glassner, Bill Froehlich, David Braff; they hired a bunch of guild writers and so the guys who were there to get them started, we got nothing. The only reason I continued to have a relationship with them was because I had a relationship with Gil, and Gil was the show's producer.

GA: And the only reason I had a relationship with them was because Bob came to me and asked me to do the show. My initial reaction as a producer was, had we not had the meeting at the Chateau Marmont, and had it in somebody's office, we probably could have afforded to pay the writers a little bit more money.

AK: That's probably True. *Freddy's Nightmares* was a strange show in every way, shape and form.

GA: Ten pages per day, five days per episode, the next day do another one, and we did them consistently, that was year one. The second year, the same thing only with more of a mandate to break them down into half-hours, hours and two-hours.

The irony of the story, cut to: a few years later I get this call about *Tales from the Crypt*. I go in to see Joel Silver and Dick Donner about the show and Joel is pacing in front of the desk and he says, "It has to look like a movie, can't look like television, gotta look like a movie." I'm sitting there thinking, I don't even know what the hell he's talking about, what's the difference? And then he says, "And every day you have to shoot five pages, every day, day in and day out. You think you can do that?" I remember looking at him and saying, "Uh, what do we do after lunch?" He got really mad at me and started yelling and I said, "No, no, I just did this show, *Freddy's Nightmares*, I was shooting ten pages a day. You're saying I have to shoot five pages a day, I think I can do that before lunch."

Freddy's Nightmares was sort of a training ground before going on to *Tales from the Crypt* and being able to figure out how we were going to make that show even better than we had done on *Freddy's Nightmares*. We had a little bit more resources, but not much.

AK: We've talked about this on our podcast, about how Greg Melton was really the secret sauce. Greg's ability to create sets, and in fact, systems that Greg had created just to pull off *Freddy's Nightmares* became part of how we did *Tales from the Crypt*. We had a night crew building sets, we became a twenty-four hour operation, it was the only way to do it. *Freddy's Nightmares* was my first produced work. I remember being on the set the very first day of production and feeling kind of awed by it all. It was quite surreal.

GA: It was for me too. I had made some other smaller shows and movies, so I at least, kind of knew what a camera was, and I could point to the camera as opposed to the light. It was a very interesting experience for us just in terms of sort of learning and doing, doing and learning, all at the same time.

HC: On the show, did you ever have any of the directors break down from the sheer amount of demand for the episodes?

GA: Almost every episode. We would have directors who would, say, after the first hour they would have gotten three shots and we had planned forty shots or thirty shots for the day. They would come to us and say, "We can't do this, we're never going to get there." Alan and I would look at each other and say, "We are. We have to. We don't have a choice. Its not like we're trying to punish you any more than they (the producers) are punishing us. We have to finish the day's work, we don't have any money to go any further." If we had more money, believe me, we'd be the first guys to have said, "Hey, take another hour, or two, or three, or ten." But there just wasn't that luxury. So yeah, we were dealing with that all the time.

Looking back on it, the show was probably a great experience, a learning experience for us which we used a lot on *Tales from the Crypt*, as to how to construct material and how to shoot. Especially on *Tales from the Crypt*, we were able to go to the directors, even some of the bigger names like John Frankenheimer or Billy Friedkin and say to them, "What about doing it this way, or that way?"

I tell this story on our podcast about Tobe Hooper on an episode of *Tales from the Crypt* that Alan and I wrote. Tobe got into a problem and as opposed to being a typical asshole producer and saying, "Well, I'm closing you down in six hours and you've got to figure this out," I looked at him and said, "Tobe, relax. Have lunch, I'm gonna go upstairs and Alan and I are gonna talk it over and I'll come back down in twenty minutes with a plan. If you like the plan, do it. If you don't like it, I'm not gonna argue with you, I'm gonna go back upstairs and we will come up with another plan, but suffice it to say, we gotta finish the day's work today." Sometimes that makes for better storytelling, and we ultimately came up with a better plan and it worked. I think we wouldn't have been able to do as good as we did had we not had that experience on *Freddy's Nightmares*. On that show, we were up against it, every day. Every day was a run for your money and every day when we said wrap, Alan and I just about collapsed.

AK: The executive producers were quite shocked that we could do what we did with the resources that we had. But when we went into the next season of *Tales from the Crypt*, did they reward us by giving back the million dollars that we had made up for? No. There was a point on that season, because they had cut our budget back, we always shot *Tales from the Crypt* episodes in five days and we wound up having to shoot some in four days. The first director that we pulled a day from was Russell Mulcahy. Russell got very upset, but he's such a pro and such a trooper that he came back with a great episode. He's such a great visual director that he plowed it into just innovating clever ways to combine this action to that action. The strange thing is, when you take creative people and you take away the money and the time and you force them to be more creative, most of the time they are. And ultimately, they suffer for it, there's no reward.

DD: In the *Freddy's Nightmares* episode, "Love Stinks," Gil, you have a cameo in a pizza oven. Was that planned or did someone just not show up that day?

GA: Well, let me answer that by saying that I wasn't wearing makeup. It was planned, I don't know why we did it, but it was planned. It was someone's idea, I don't remember who, it wasn't my idea. It might have been the director, but yeah, someone just wanted me to be in the oven.

HC: *Tales from the Crypt* is very well loved, and rightfully so, but *Freddy's Nightmares* is kind of the bastard son of a thousand maniacs.

AK: Well, there was something kind of cynical at the creation of the show.

HC: Do you think that perhaps *Freddy's Nightmares* would have been more successful had marijuana been legal in most of the United States?

AK: As someone who is a start of the day until the end of the day marijuana smoker, I'm not saying no. I think it was cerebral because it had to be. Yeah, it would have been easier to create episodes of *Freddy's Nightmares* hopped up on dope because, you know, that's how I write anyway. You can think so many different levels at the same time, it just makes it easier. That's why guys like Louis Armstrong smoked dope to create jazz. It's not a coincidence, it really is very conducive to the creative process. It couldn't have hurt.

DD: Are there any stories from the pilot episode that you can share?

GA: Tobe, from *Freddy's Nightmares* became somewhat of a friend, but after the episode of *Tales from the Crypt*, we became very close friends. We talked probably every two or three days from that point on. I guess our mutual respect for one another just grew, and that started with *Freddy's Nightmares.*

I know initially when I first brought him on to do the show, he was frightened about the ten pages a day and how we only had five days to shoot. Tobe was addicted to Dr. Pepper and I would say to him, "I have a case of Dr. Pepper and its chilled. You can have it any time you like." He would always offer it to me and I'm like, "No, no, those are for you. I don't need to be hyped up on caffeine, I'm hyped up enough."

So when we got on *Tales from the Crypt*, I had Dr. Pepper there for him. One day I said to him, "I got a whole case and there's still eight left, I don't understand." Tobe replied, Well, you know, I kind of switched to sugar free." I said, "Why didn't you tell me this? I could have gotten the sugar free." But that was the kind of guy that Tobe was. He was just the sweetest guy in the world.

To make horror and do all these scary things, and to make *Texas Chainsaw Massacre*, you'd think, oh my god, how does this guy think? Where's his mind? And his mind was just that of one of the sweetest guys I have ever known. He was just a really decent person, and there's probably not a day that goes by that I don't miss him.

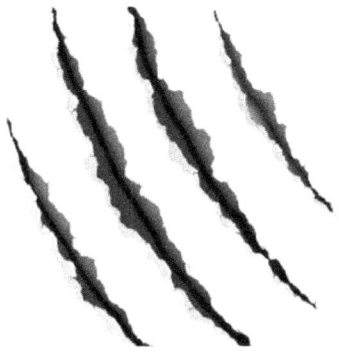

JEFF FREILICH

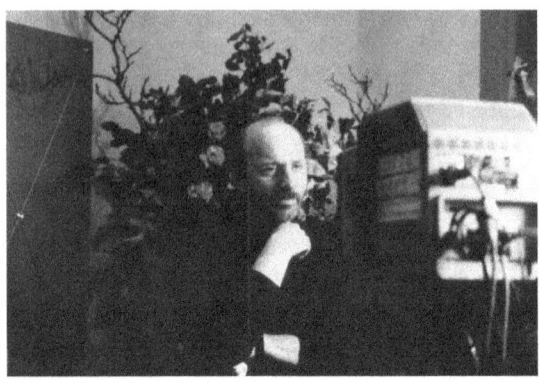

Jeff Freilich is an American film and television producer, writer and director. Freilich studied psychology at Antioch University in Yellow Springs Ohio and medicine at the University of Southern California. He began his professional writing career working under Roger Corman at New World Pictures. Freilich's television writing career began in 1975 with an episode of *Doctor's Hospital* and producing with one episode of *The Incredible Hulk* in 1979.

Freilich would continue writing and producing through the years, more recently producing the AMC hit series *Halt and Catch Fire.* Freilich began directing television in 1987 with six episodes of *Falcon Crest* before moving on to direct one episode of *Freddy's Nightmares*, a show that he helped develop and executive produce. After *Freddy's Nightmares*, Freilich would create the CBS show *Dark Justice*. Other television directing credits include *Burn Notice* and *Halt and Catch Fire*.

**Interview conducted by
Henrique Couto and David Denoyer**

HC: We would love to talk to you about how you got your start, you've had such an interesting career both pre and post *Freddy's Nightmares*. How did it all start?

JF: I grew up in the Upper West Side of Manhattan and a couple of my closest friends were sons of celebrated, but blacklisted screenwriters. One was Tim Hunter, who's father Ian McLellan Hunter, had received the Oscar for *Roman Holiday*, but was later blacklisted as he had basically fronted the screenplay for Dalton Trumbo, who was very close friends with the Hunters. Ian was a terrific guy who helped mentor me as a writer, he wrote my student speeches when I would run for student government. I would go to Tim's house and Ian and I would read the speech and make it so good that only the teachers liked it. The other close friend was Jimmy Lardner, who was Ring Lardner Jr.'s son, who had won the Oscar for a movie called *Woman of the Year*. Twenty-nine years later after going to jail as one of the "Hollywood Ten," finally got another crack at writing with his own name for the Robert Altman film *M*A*S*H*, for which he won another Oscar at the age of 58. Between my friends Jimmy and Tim and Johnny Caplan, who really wanted to be a filmmaker, and a couple other people who were part of that Upper West Side film community, that was our poker game. Tim and I became best friends and I had told everybody that I was going to be a doctor, so every adult that I knew was proud and felt secure that I was going to be taken care of.

I went to the wrong school for that, I applied to a bunch of colleges, got into a few, but I loved the idea of Antioch College, which was a small and politically, quite radical school, in Yellow Springs, Ohio. When we were there, the school had thirty-five hundred students, in a town with a population of about one thousand, the town itself was mostly students and most of the stores on the main streets were for students and if you drove or rode a bicycle you could go a couple miles out of town to the dairy and get fresh ice cream, beyond that there wasn't much there. I went to Antioch because I was attracted to the work study program, it was a five year college with no vacations, except maybe two weeks over Christmas. In those five years, every year you spent six months working somewhere in either three month blocks or six month blocks. The idea was that you'd take a job either in the areas that best led you toward your career goal, or in areas that you wanted to become familiar with.

I had a variety of different jobs and while I was there I made some films and ran the film society. We had a two thousand seat auditorium, it was fantastic with great 35mm arc projection, and we also had a very wonderful movie theater in town called the Little Art, it was the closest thing to a cinematheque that you could find. Keep in mind, I went to college from 1964 to 1969, so it was just at the beginning of the Vietnam War, the protests, the women's movement, launched by the Equal Rights Amendment. It was a very volatile time, but at the same time it was an incredibly idyllic place to be and I spent a lot of my time making and showing films. I also started a film festival that rivaled the one in Ann Arbor, Michigan, because my best friend, Tim Hunter had gone off to Harvard and had started the Harvard Film Society Film Festival there, so we would share films, I showed all of Tim's original films which starred his roommate, Tommy Lee Jones.

Ultimately, I went on to medical school, I really had no desire at that point to get into the film industry. You have to remember, there were no film schools, NYU was just about to open up the Tisch film school and AFI was just an idea. There really was no interest in learning, academically, about film, and film is expensive.

We had to make film on film and the average student couldn't afford to make a movie. It was something that only very special people were dedicated to. I had several friends at Antioch who went off and helped the Maysles brothers make *Gimme Shelter.* Julia Reichert, the great documentary filmmaker, was in that class. Those were serious filmmakers, I was not that person. I made a take on Jean Luc Goddard called *Waiting for Goddard*, I made a kind of a jungle movie based on a series of films that we would show at this Saturday night film festival that we would get as stoned and drunk as we could and go to called the Festival of Garbage.

While I was at Antioch, one day I walked into the union building and on the wall there was a sign up sheet for an alumnus who was teaching a course for writing for film and television. It didn't say anything about who it was or what the course was and so nobody signed up for it. I did, and ultimately was one of about six people who finally signed up. The course was being held in the auditorium, which was ridiculous for only six of us, and onto the stage walked Rod Serling. He looked exactly like he did on the beginning of *The Twilight Zone*, and he said, "Well, I guess everyone who wants to learn to write came. Why don't you all move forward?" For a period of several weeks there was kind of a symposium where he would comment on things that we wrote and give assignments, and that was kind of the beginning of it. What I got more out of those days more than anything else were rules to live by in writing. One of my favorites was that every dramatic scene is an argument and the first question you ask yourself is why are both sides right. That's what dramatic tension is about. The other thing that Serling said, that a later writing partner of mine reinforced was that what you write should mean something.

So, I applied to a bunch of medical schools, got into a few, but USC was two things: first of all, it was as far away from my parents in New York that I could get, and the other thing was that it was in California. My friend, Tim, was starting off at the American Film Institute, which was brand new at the time, so it gave me an opportunity to spend time with Tim who was the only person that I knew in town. At the end of the first year, I left med school and went to AFI and produced Tim's thesis film, which starred Bob Random and Charles McGraw. I got a taste for the business as a producer and went to George Stevens Jr. and asked, "What do I need to know about producing?" He said, "You're gonna have $25,000, make the movie for that, period." It was forty-five minutes and it was ambitious, and we did. But, I went back to med school after that, before finally deciding that I really just wanted to write.

I wrote a screenplay that really wasn't very good, and then I wrote a couple of other things. Because of my relationship with Tim, I met Christoper Trumbo, Dalton Trumbo's son, and Chris and I became very quick friends. He was partnered with a writer named Michael Butler, who was Hugo Butler's son, another blacklisted writer. Michael and Chris took a particular interest in me and they were offered two feature films at the same time, one was called *The Dawn is Dead,* for Hal Wallace, and the other was called *Paradise Flats*, which was a Western to be shot in Mexico by a very famous Mexican director called José Bolaños. They couldn't do both at the same time so they got ahold of José and said, "Listen, we'll guarantee this young writer's work. Let him write it and we will give him notes and help him rewrite."

I was a huge fan of Sergio Leone and so my approach to Westerns was very little dialogue and mostly shot descriptions, so that's what I wrote. Chris and Michael, who had been writing mostly feature films and some television wanted it to read more like one of those and by the time I was done with my second draft based on them, it was a very talk-y Western. I sent it down to Mexico City and never heard back, so I called José a few weeks later. He said, "It's not what I thought it would be, the way you described it to me…" I said, "Listen, I wrote another draft before Chris and Michael got their hands on it. Let me send you that." I did and he responded with tickets to Mexico City and wanted me to come down not only to do a re-write on that but do other things. He loved it, it was exactly what he wanted. I get to Mexico City and José meets me in the lobby of a hotel and takes me upstairs. He had a handful of keys and he opened up a door and said, "This is where you'll sleep," he opens another one, "This is where you'll work," another one, "This is where you can entertain guests," another, "This is where you can put all of your things, and the other room, why should anyone else share your floor?" That was my baptism of fire.

I came back to Los Angeles and eventually worked with Tim Hunter and Roger Corman at New World Pictures. Joe Dante had called Tim because they were having some problems with the dialogue for the film, *Hollywood Boulevard*. Tim reached out to me because they needed a lot of punch up and extra stuff, and Tim and I went in together on it. What I learned at Roger's was that anything can be made for anything if you put your mind to it. Money is not a measure of quality or talent.

Later I was contacted by a rich kid that I knew at Antioch and he wanted me to write a movie because he liked the student films I had made. It didn't get made, but it got to an agent named Bill Hart, who was a former agent for William Morris, and he called me for a meeting. I took the meeting because I was desperate for money, I had defaulted on my med school loans and I told him that I need to write something that pays me tomorrow. He said, "Television. That's the quickest way to make money, and as a writer it's one of the most satisfying things to do because you actually get to see it made." Bill got me a meeting for a new series called *Doctor's Hospital* because I had been to med school. I pitched a bunch of ideas and executives turned to the writer and said, "He's gonna have your job soon." That's what began my television career. After *Doctor's Hospital,* I started scrounging around for more television and that got me to *Beretta*. I wrote a script and turned it in and the day after, Robert Blake himself called me and said, "Kid, come in, you're coming to work for me."

That was for me, a very stressful period. I was under pressure all the time, I was doing horrible things to my body, I was taking things both to keep me awake and asleep. Finally I decided to leave the business, I left *Beretta* and moved up to Oregon. Finally when I was thirty, I said to myself, it's time to grow up, so I moved back to Los Angeles and went back to Bill Hart, my first agent. I ended up with a one year TV deal at Universal and was back in the business. After working at Universal, I went back to features and wrote a comedy at Disney which was called *Two Scoops* for Bill Murray. Murray at that time decided not to do comedy and instead went on to do *Razor's Edge*. I then went back to TV at a company called Lorimar, a company that I worked at for fourteen years. Every year I would work on pilots, a couple of them sold, a lot of them didn't. Even still, it was a wonderful experience for me.

It was during that time that I wound up being what would now be called a showrunner. In the 1980's when the nighttime soap opera hit, television changed dramatically, serializing shows became much more attractive. *Dallas, Knot's Landing* and *Falcon Crest* were the three shows that Lorimar had. Earl Hamner Jr. had created *Falcon Crest* and when he was ready to retire he wanted me to take over after the fifth season. I basically told them that I wanted to be the highest paid person on the show, that I wanted no notes from Lorimar, and also none from CBS either. Lee Rich said to me, "Fuck CBS, if they're such geniuses everything they put on the air would be a hit. If you do what they tell you to do and it fails, they're gonna blame you. If you do what you want and it succeeds, they're gonna take the credit anyway. So, fuck them, I'll keep them away from you." How can you say no to that? I basically wanted to make *Vertigo* for twenty-eight episodes, so we went and got Kim Novak to help realize that. There was this one kind of magical day when a producer called me up from the set and said that the director hadn't shown up, his car had broken down in San Diego and everyone was just standing around. It was an episode that I had written and they needed somebody to direct, so he said, "Why don't you do it?"

After *Falcon Crest* and during the middle of the WGA strike, I got a call from Lorimar, who at that time was merging with a non-union company called Telepictures, they asked me to come in to discuss a new project. Along with New Line Cinema, they thought it would be a good idea to make *Nightmare on Elm Street* into a syndicated television show. They wanted me to come up with an idea and I said, "I can't do that, there's a writers strike going on right now." Well, they had already put together a group of non-union people to come up with stories and scripts. They had brought in Scott Stone to produce it, they brought in Gil Adler, and they had enlisted the reluctant help of feature writer, Jonathan Betuel, who had written *The Last Starfighter*. They had a bunch of these non-union scripts and they asked me to read them which I did and they were horrible. Nobody knew what to do with Freddy, they made him into like a stand up comic and the stories were horrible.

I wasn't really a fan of horror, but I loved Wes Craven's original film and the second one as well. The reason was because they had an underpinning of reality that to have dreams haunt you and manifest themselves in reality, was terrifying. We all have those dreams, everyone has had the fear of death in a dream, and here was something that tapped into that basic human fear. The question is, what do you do as a television show? So I went back to my roots which were Rod Serling and *The Twilight Zone*, and I came up with the idea that what we would do is have Freddy Krueger introduce the shows, to introduce what the fear element of the story was. Then we would know that Freddy is going to have something to do with that person's nightmare. I agreed to meet with Bob Shaye to talk conceptually, but with the strike going on, I wasn't willing to do anything beyond that. I wanted to know what the rules were because I had heard that Bob was very concerned that we were going to ruin his legacy. Bob was concerned about overusing Freddy for television and that people wouldn't want to spend the money to come to the theaters. I kind of had to make a deal with him about how much we could actually use Freddy as a character in the show like he is in the movies.

The strike was ending and now I was willing to meet with writers, but real writers, not the people who had written the bad scripts, I wanted to bring in writers that I knew. Jon Betuel was a friend and so he kind of became my right hand man, who was the supervising producer. I was the executive producer along with Bob Shaye, we shared that credit. I insisted on making the entire show union for SAG, DGA and writer's guild, but stayed non-union for the crew, which we were allowed to do because Scott Stone had a sort of non-union agreement. This was the only way that we could make the show for a half million dollars an hour, which to put into perspective, is less than ten percent of what the average hour of television costs today. Dick Robertson was the president of Warner Brothers Syndication, and he was telling me that what they really wanted was to be able to split the show into half-hours later on down the line. I said, "That's impossible, as a writer, I don't know how you do that. What you're asking me to make is forty-four episodes that each take two to three days to shoot that each cost a quarter of a million dollars." He said, "I guess that's what I'm asking." I walked out of the office feeling hopeless, but by the time I got home I had an idea: What if we hire the same writer, same director and same cast to play two different stories? That's a start.

Now the conundrum was how do you make forty-four episodes out of twenty-two hours? How do you preserve the same cast? How do you keep the same director at it? What we found ourselves doing was that we'd alternate from show to show depending on what set we were on. In "Missing Persons" for example, it was first the babysitter's story which is a girl's fear of her eating disorder, the second was a guy trapped in a life that he didn't like. The plant that I put in the beginning of that episode was that the guy was very flirtatious when he opens the door and sees the babysitter. It's the old trope of the dad and the babysitter, but really it was to be paid off in the second half hour where she becomes the noir model to his kind of underworld type guy who was trapped in this car accident. The story was really about your life flashing before your eyes as you die from a car accident.

That became a really difficult problem to solve on an ongoing basis, but I had really good people around me. Especially, Jon Betuel, Jill Donner, who brought a much needed female perspective, and Michael DeLuca. Mike was kind of fresh out of Tisch and was working doing odd different things creatively for Bob Shaye. Bob took a liking to him and Mike became like his surrogate son. Mike and I had become very close because Bob had said, "Take Mike, he's a walking encyclopedia of *Nightmare on Elm Street*. He'll also know what we are planning to do, so if you come up with an idea that we've either done or are planning to do, he can tell you to go a different direction. He can help preserve the legacy and the franchise, and at the same time, he's a geek for this stuff." I wasn't, for me, I was more into fantasy, either *One Step Beyond* or *The Twilight Zone*, stuff like that. I was never really into horror until I did this show. But, I was a good storyteller so I could come up with good ways to kill people. There are rules in genre and if you break those rules, the audience is very savvy and they realize and resent it. I wanted to serve the audience as well as I could.

Mike spent a lot of time with me and I quickly learned what a genius he was. We started to become a sort of team, and together we came up with the story for the pilot episode that we brought David Erhman in to write. David was the brother-in-law of Tim Hunter, the whole thing is circular, this is the most incestuous business of all time. The story though, was ours and we had to get permission from Bob Shaye. Bob loved the idea to do the genesis story because no one had ever done it before. The real score though, was Tobe Hooper. The man who made the original *Texas Chainsaw Massacre,* you can't beat him. Tobe is going to come in with the exact sensibility that you need to do this. The only problem with Tobe Hooper was that he didn't know that a day only lasts twenty-four hours. A normal shooting day was supposed to last twelve to fourteen hours and we would work eighteen to twenty hours. There was one day when the entire crew showed up on set in black armbands because they had been working such long hours. I made the decision to give them all Friday off and pay them for it.

DeLuca, Betuel and I were the ones who really guided the show. And the joy of having someone like Gil Adler, who was so tapped into those low budget and horror people, was that he helped channel toward us people like Ken Wiederhorn, Mick Garris, John Lafia, George Kaczender, really wonderful directors. Some of them even went on to direct episodes of a series I created after *Freddy's Nightmares* called *Dark Justice*. The carrot that I gave each of these directors was, "Make your own version of it. I'm not going to tell you what to shoot, I'm not going to tell you that what you're shooting is wrong, that you can't change the script, and I'm going to give you as close to a final cut that you can get as long as its down to time. Come and make your own movie." It was a combination of Gil Adler's connections and Bob Shaye who did some incredible backroom negotiating with people who owed him favors. For example, our production designer, Mick Strawn, he had designed *Nightmare on Elm Street 4*. There was a list of people who came from the *Nightmare on Elm Street* side, as well as other directors who were willing to work with Bob Shaye because he could give them a feature.

In the meantime, DeLuca had become a better writer, but he was also intent on getting New Line to do more than just *Nightmare on Elm Street*. He would find scripts in the trash where readers had just thrown them out and he would take them to Bob and say, "I think we should make this." *Boogie Nights* is a good example, *Teenage Mutant Ninja Turtles,* and ultimately it was Mike who convinced Bob to buy *Lord of the Rings* and to make all three at the same time.

That was how we made *Freddy's Nightmares*, it was a lot of talented people working at a breakneck pace. Necessity being the mother of invention is not only a cliché, but a truth because a lot of what you see there, almost everything we did was practical special effects. It was like making an indie film in the era of Roger Corman and borrowing people from their very well traveled sets. People with a lot of experience adding inventive ways of doing things for no money, and who took great pleasure in doing that. The studio we shot in was this little shack in the middle of the valley next to a bar. It was a rundown warehouse that was really never used for movie making, it may have been used for porn for all I know, but I can't be certain of that. DeLuca and I would go next door during shooting and have a drink, play pool and come up with ideas. Then we would go back on set to see how it was going. I always felt that directors and actors were better without parental supervision so we left them as alone as possible.

I left *Freddy's Nightmares* after the first season to become a consultant on the show. After doing twenty-two episodes, forty-four half hours, I was getting to the point where my mind was in such a dark place because every day I would wake up and think of more and more grotesque things to do to people, and that's what I was totally preoccupied with all of the time. On one hand, I wanted to move on to something new and different and fresh, and on the other, it was a really difficult job. It was a lot of hours, I never really got to see my family at all, it was far, far away from where I lived so the commute was two hours round trip, and then we'd go work for fourteen to sixteen hours. Talk about not having a life.

So, I was off developing a new show for CBS and they wanted to fill the 11:00 PM slot with, instead of a talk show, an hour of what they called "Crimetime." "Crimetime, after Primetime," that's what it's called. They had me come in with the executive vice president of Lorimar and I pitched an idea for a show and they gave me an order for twenty-two episodes in the room, without ever reading a pilot. They said, "Just go make a great show." What the catch was, is that it was at a reduced license fee and he thought that would scare me, but as it turns out having just come off of *Freddy's Nightmares*, nothing was cheaper than that show. I knew, based on my experience on *Freddy's Nightmares*, what the limitations of writing would be and I also realized that I needed to put together a writing staff that had very few people, because I couldn't afford a lot of writers, and we would do the same thing that we did on *Freddy's Nightmares*. I reached out to the people that I had the most respect and creative admiration for and number one on the list was Mike DeLuca.

I called Mike and said, "Look, I've got this new show, would you come on as an executive story consultant?" He said, "I can't leave Bob." I said, "You know what, I'm not asking you to leave Bob. Are you there all the time at New Line?" "No." I said,

"Would you be available to do some consulting work when we have story meetings?" "Sure." I said, "Would you be available to write or rewrite some of these scripts?" "Sure." I said, "Because your sensibility, your storytelling would be invaluable to the show." I told him what the show was and he loved it. The second person I called was James Cappe, who I had met on *Freddy's Nightmares* through Jonathan Betuel. Jay wrote two wonderful scripts and had become a friend of mine, and its like, I'd love to spend a year in a room with Jay Cappe. The third person at the time was a guy named Duke Sandfer who I had known and worked with in the past. And ultimately, I brought Chris Trumbo on board as well, it was a very small group.

The show was called *Dark Justice*. When the pilot aired at 11:00 PM on a Friday night I got a call from Bob Shaye at 12:15 AM, he said,"So you pay homage to your big friend DeLuca and you hire him and you don't mention me at all?" The thing that hadn't been discussed yet was what was Mike DeLuca doing with a credit on your show? I said, "Look, this is what I'm paying him," which was a lot more than Bob was paying him, Mike managed to buy his house with the first year's *Dark Justice* money. I said, "He's brilliant. Are you missing him? Is he not doing his job?" "No, no, he's great, he's amazing." I said, "So, what's the problem?" The next thing I know, DeLuca comes to me and asks, "What did you say to Shaye?" I said, "What are you talking about?" "He just made me vice president of New Line." Each year Mike did a little bit less physical participation on *Dark Justice* and by the time the show was done after three seasons, Mike DeLuca was president of New Line. It was like a tug of war between me and Bob because we both recognized his talent.

A lot of people kind of grew up on *Freddy's Nightmares* and got their start there. Tom DeSimone directed a lot of Freddy's Nightmares, he was largely a gay porn director before that show. The combination of these new very talented people in an atmosphere that had very few restrictions and rules also made us less picky about who we hired sometimes. Very often I would hire directors based on a personality test, we would sit and talk and if I liked somebody, great. DeSimone was terrific and talking to him I realized, what's the difference between my working for Roger Corman and his making gay porn? He was a film lover, all he ever wanted to do was to make movies, so he went in the direction that he could. It was the only thing he was allowed to make at the time, nobody else wanted to hire him until we brought him onto *Freddy's Nightmares*. Tom could shoot a twelve hour day and make it a really good show. He knew exactly what shots he needed, he knew how to take one shot and make it into five shots so he wouldn't have to keep moving the camera around. He was just really pleasant to everyone and he gave the actors really cogent, thoughtful notes, character based goal motivated notes. That is an art form in itself, especially in television, you don't have the number of takes, the time, the rehearsals, any of those tools that you have in features to be able to craft a performance. You're really doing it on the fly, so you have to be really careful about the words that you use.

For me, that was *Freddy's Nightmares*. The bad news, although it turned into good news because it ultimately gave birth to a new generation of fans, was that I found out that the show was airing at 6:00 PM on a Sunday night in Philadelphia of all places. It was like, I told them at Warner Brothers that this was an adult show and needed to be aired late at night. Instead, they went ahead and aired it all around the country at different times. The very principle of *Nightmare on Elm Street* is that Springwood is a town where the teenagers have been completely abandoned by the adults. It's the nightmares of the teenagers, not the adults. What I learned was that if you're telling the stories about teenage fears then you can't restrict the audience to only people who are over eighteen, or only adults who watch TV at eleven at night. So we had to kind of be true to that original premise of *Nightmare on Elm Street*. My theory was that the reason that the kids in this town were having nightmares was because they were basically abandoned and abused, not physically, but mentally abused by their parents.

I love telling stories and I have been fortunate enough to work with such great directors and filmmakers, show makers and actors. People have asked me what's my favorite thing that I have done or what part of my career was the highlight. There is nothing more fun for me than looking back. I tell people that one day I want to be sitting on the porch at the motion picture retirement home drinking a gin and tonic and saying, "I remember that person, I gave that person their start. Look at what that person did." There is no way anybody can ever tell you, in all honesty, that they got where they are on their own. Always let everyone have a voice, because the quietest voice could be the most important.

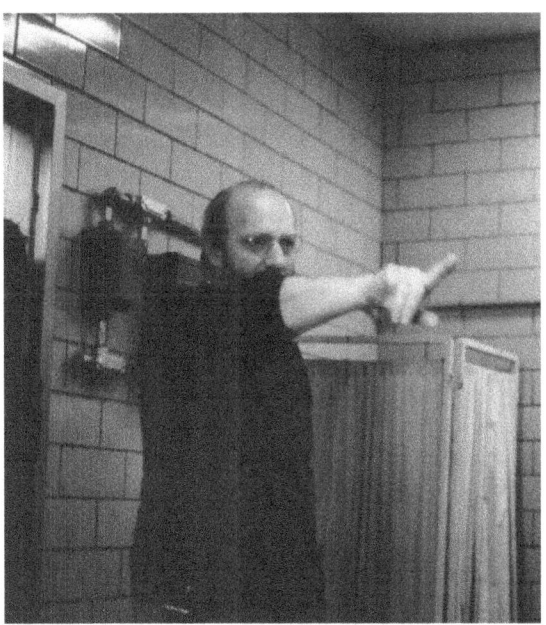

MICK STRAWN

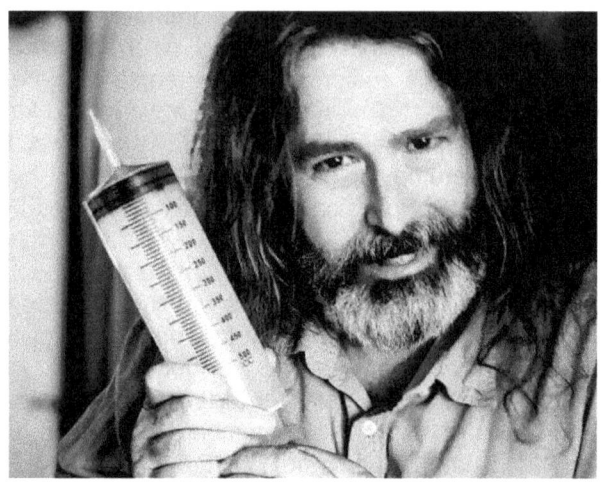

Mick Strawn is an American production designer, art director and special effects artist. Mick started in the film business as a construction coordinator for the film *Breakin' 2: Electric Boogaloo*. He would go on to work in the art department on *Tales from the Darkside, Critters 2*, the 1992 film version of *Buffy the Vampire Slayer* and *Candyman* among others. Mick is also credited as a special effects artist for the films *Witchboard, The Kindred, 8 Heads in a Duffel Bag, Boogie Nights* and *Blade*. Mick is perhaps best known as a production designer, having designed the films *The Hidden, A Nightmare on Elm Street 4: The Dream Master, Leatherface: Texas Chainsaw Massacre III, Revenge of the Nerds III: The Next Generation* and many others. Strawn served as the production designer for *Freddy's Nightmares* for season one of the show.

Interview conducted by
Henrique Couto and David Denoyer

HC: Having done *Nightmare on Elm Street 4*, how did you end up on *Freddy's Nightmares*? Were you asked by New Line? How did that kind of happen?

MS: I was told to go protect it. Literally. They said, "Go protect our interests."

HC: That makes perfect sense especially because on an anthology television series, production design is pretty important, you can't reusue that much.

MS: I have to tell you, honestly, you are always seeing the same flats over and over again. In fact they would get so fucking heavy from all of the paint. They would get so heavy that we would have to take them outside and cut them up. You think I'm kidding about that, there could literally have been some flats in there that would have been painted over forty times. Forty coats of paint makes an eight foot long flat tough to pick up. You have to understand that absolutely everybody that worked on the *Nightmare on Elm Street* films and the TV show were all working at way above our normal capacity.

DD: In 1985-1986 you had worked on ten episodes of *Tales from the Darkside*, how did that experience compare to your later work on *Freddy's Nightmares*?

MS: That show was kind of like a step up production-wise, even though *Tales from the Darkside* was a lower budget show than *Freddy's Nightmares.* Gideon Porath shot the episodes that I was on.

DD: Could you give us a little more on what a production designer on a film set does? What exactly is the task at hand?

MS: Some people define it pretty narrowly, a production designer as being the one who oversees the art department and kind of makes sure that it's tied in to wardrobe and props to create the overall look of the film. I have always gone a lot further than that, I'll go out and start haranguing the writers if I don't get my way. I tell people this, if you look at *Batman*, you know that every bit of that film was made, was created, the look of it, everything, that's a production designer's job. *Batman* is the perfect example because there's the batmobile, his costume and all that. All of that comes together to make a new and different world. The thing that you don't know is that there is a production designer behind all of that. A production designer pulls all of these things together, especially on *Freddy's Nightmares,* I was the one who was kind of doing the effects with Andre and trying to teach him and I kept bringing in people who were beginners in the industry. It was one of those shows where in order to keep a construction crew and a swing crew to move set dressings and construction stuff in and out was very difficult. That set was open twenty-four hours, I would come in early in the morning so that I could bed them in and get the filming crew in, then I would go home for a while and come back in and work maybe from like ten at night until two in the morning. Almost every day, we turned around two sets. It was a small warehouse, so we divided it into four sections so that two sets could be active while we were working on the other two and it just kept going day after day after day. We would have this meeting every Friday about the upcoming show, which we would immediately start in on. At least every other script they would have Freddy bursting into flames and the thing was, A - we couldn't afford to do that and B - it would have been really boring. I remember one time the key grip looked up and said, "Couldn't we just have Freddy burst into song instead?"

DD: One thing we have come to love is that with the intros and outros to the epi-

-sodes you have Freddy talking to you each time and it seems like they are always trying to one-up each other.

MS: It's the lunacy of doing things at three o'clock in the morning. The thing is, the Freddy's domain stuff was pretty tongue-in-cheek. Any fucking thing we could come up with, we would do. Robert would come and hang out, he and I had known each other for years by that point, I introduced him to his wife, his wife worked for me on a show called *Frankenstein: The College Years*, my magnum opus. So, Robert and I had been hanging around together off and on for an awful long time.

HC: I wanted to mention, here in our studio is a poster for a movie that you worked on called *Night of the Scarecrow*, the Jeff Burr film.

MS: *Night of the Scarecrow*! Jeff Burr was friends with the fucking world. Jeff and I had been friends for years, we did *Texas Chainsaw Massacre III* together. I moved to Tennessee and when I got out here to Nashville, we would see each other at conventions all the time. A good friend of mine is R.A. Mihailoff, he and Jeff were bonded as friends forever. I just recently designed a film called *Pig Hill* which was executive produced by R.A., Jeff was actually supposed to direct it but he was having health issues and the film ended up being directed by Kevin Lewis who had done *Willy's Wonderland*. Its like, my life has been Jeff Burr adjacent for so many years, I just can't tell you. My heart is still completely broken that he passed.

DD: You are credited as the manager and miniature director for the Roger Corman produced film *The Fantastic Four*, we would love to hear more about that.

MS: And the production designer! I never know what to say about that one. A guy calls me up in the middle of November and says, "I have a film, it's a Marvel film." This was before Marvel films were a thing so I had to say, "What the fuck is a Marvel film?" He says, "Well, it's *The Fantastic Four* from the comic book. Here's the thing, we need half of it shot before January 1st." I go down and meet with them and Oley Sassone, who was the director and we sit around and I said, "I can't imagine what it would take to put this together in such a short period of time." And then I dove in and we did it! I knew from the beginning why the film was made. I think some of the actors really believed that this was going to be their magnum opus as it were. I never believed that but I did the best that I could on Roger Corman's little lot, which was a modified lumber yard. We had to have half of it done and I built it out with sets and I remember going over to where we had the lair, which I thought was a really cool set and I'm locking up for the few days that we had off since we had made it halfway before the end of the year. There was an old man sitting up on the stage, he was sitting there on a folding chair that he had pulled up and he had a legal pad in front of him. I said, "Hey, I gotta lock up here, you gotta leave because I have to get it locked up and I'm tired." Let's face it, as a low budget production designer, I was always tired. He said, "That's OK, I have the key, I'll lock it up. I like your set here, I just gotta make some notes."

He introduced himself as Roger, I said that I was Mick and he said, "I know who you are." I get back on January 4th and found out that that son of a bitch was in the process of writing a film when I interrupted him, he was writing a film about that set. What I didn't know was that they had literally started filming the next morning. They literally filmed another film on my set, and repainted them while we were gone. I was furious, we had put up the tape that said "HOT SET DO NOT CROSS." How can you expect to get another job in Hollywood if you cross the tape that said "HOT SET DO NOT CROSS," my mind was just completely blown.

I built a whole bunch of miniatures in my garage on the weekends while the film went along because, obviously we weren't going to need them says the CGI guy. Then on like the tenth day of the new year they came to me and said, "Do you have someone that can build some miniatures?" "Funny you should ask, the shit that you need is all in my garage right now." We brought them out and I directed it and that's it. Here's another Corman story, Corman requires that you use his equipment. The electrician comes around the corner and tells me that he just talked to the people up front saying that we needed a generator for the next set and she reaches underneath the counter and hands him a paddle, which was a really powerful distribution block that you clip on like you're jump starting a car. She says, "OK, you give the guy next door twenty bucks and then you just clip onto the power." And that was the generator. Along that vein, I needed to do some newspaper spin-ins. To do those, you have to shoot in reverse with a dowel on the end of a drill and a piece of plywood and put the newspaper on it. We're in this second unit meeting for the show and the DP goes "We're gonna need a reverse mag," because back then that was film and a reverse mag was something that would allow that type of photography. They said, "We don't have one of those," I said, "That's no problem, just turn the camera upside down." Well the DP didn't believe that it would work and wanted to just cancel those shots. I end up grabbing a three foot section of film and was demonstrating to him how it would work. I said, " Do me a favor and just put it back on the schedule." We had been filming and at the end of the day my art director walks in and sits down across from me and says, "I have been seeing the stupidest fucking thing today, and I'm one hundred percent sure that it has something to do with you because you're kind of a bastard. The thing is, there's a three foot piece of film that has been going around from person to person that they wave around and talk about how the camera is upside down, reverse this, reverse that and then they hand it to that person and they walk off with it. I know you, and I know somewhere deep down inside, that you did that."

DD: You are credited as construction manager for the film *Runaway Train*, as big fans, we would love to hear anything about the making of that film.

MS: I was doing second unit with Max Kleven who was a hero for second unit stuff. He was one of those guys that would say things like, "OK boys, this one's for the trailer!" We had to make trains to copy the trains that were in Montana and then they didn't use the trains that were in Montana because Montana had a really warm winter and they didn't get snow. The whole thing wound up being built on some wooden trains that were built on switching motors. We had to have all kinds of control of it, we had to be able to get the front piece on and off, we had to ice it, it was just so much work. We literally had a crane on another car that would come forward and lift that wreckage off of the front. I was actually in the caboose of the other train when we actually hit the caboose. It was supposed to be a model but we had to make the approach to get the two trains to look like they actually passed each other. It was a huge miscalculation, that fucking thing nailed us, it just shifted like three feet. It reminded me so much of being in California during an earthquake.

HC: Would you call *Freddy's Nightmares* one of the most challenging sets as far as time and money and resources available to you?

MS: I don't know, I have no fucking idea, it's like what they say about the '80s, if you remember them then you weren't there. It was really bad, there was this one time around Thanksgiving and we were on like, episode twenty and I was just fried. I had this Mercedes and I go home for Thanksgiving, there was a little bit of rain and I needed new wipers so they had just smeared the rain on the windshield and I just cried, that's how tired I was.

DD: One more question about *Freddy's Nightmares*, you were credited with production designer for the first season of the show, did they offer you season two at all? And what was the decision with that?

MS: Yes. I often say, if you hit your hand with a hammer, do you leave your hand in the same place? I don't know about you, but I moved my hand.

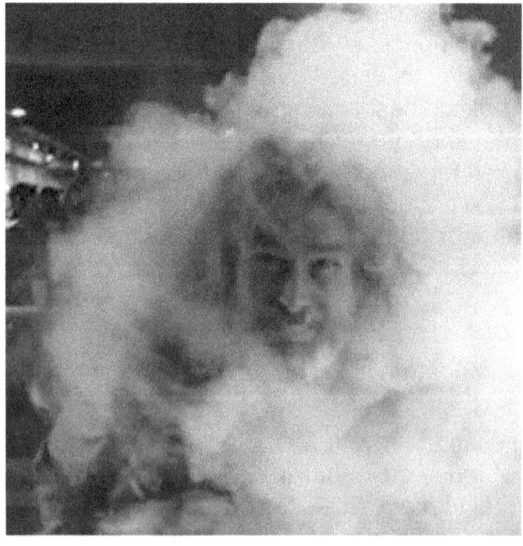

JAMES CAPPE

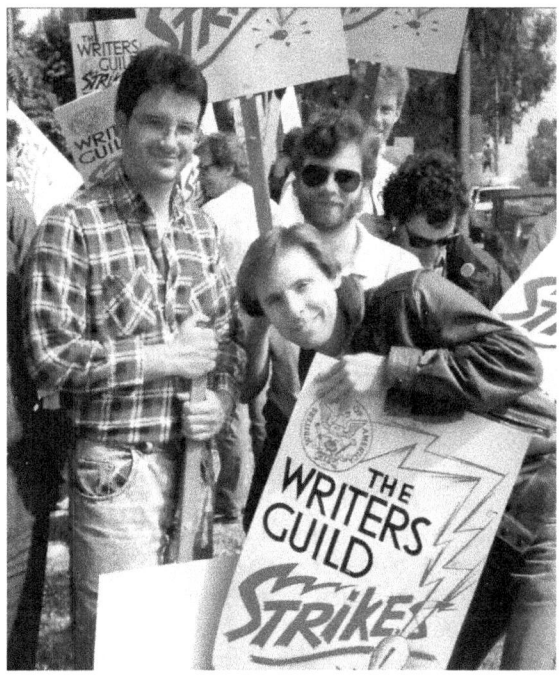

James Cappe is an American screenwriter, director and producer. In 1986, Cappe graduated from the University of Southern California's film program. Cappe got his start by writing two episodes of *Freddy's Nightmares*, "The End of the World" and "The Light at the End of the Tunnel." Cappe would go on to work as a writer, script consultant and a supervising producer of Jeff Freilich's follow-up to *Freddy's Nightmares, Dark Justice*. Cappe also wrote episodes for *Poltergeist: The Legacy* and *Mortal Kombat: Conquest*, the latter of which was also produced by New Line Television, the same studio behind *Freddy's Nightmares*.

Interview conducted by
Henrique Couto and David Denoyer

HC: Give us a little rundown of your oeuvre. What have you worked on in addition to *Freddy's Nightmares* that folks may be familiar with?

JC: My one feature film credit is *The Adventures of Ford Fairlane* which was directed by Renny Harlin, who directed *Nightmare on Elm Street 4*, and stars Robert Englund. After *Freddy's Nightmares*, I had connected with a bunch of really cool guys, most specifically, Jeff Freilich, the developer of *Freddy's Nightmares*, who kept me working over the years. My name is on about a hundred episodes of TV from the '90s. I still kept writing other stuff as well because you never know, someone might buy something.

HC: So you were born in Ohio and then later wound up in Northern California?

JC: My dad wanted to be an actor and went to New York for a little while, but then he started selling real estate and making money so we moved to Florida. Around the time that I was in the second grade we get a call from my uncle who, in a real *Beverly Hillbillies* moment said, "Y'all gotta come out here to California, it's not cold and not rainy and not humid." So we went out there and it stuck right away. I was part of this Marin County group of people, I didn't know who George Lucas was yet, but it was all a part of where I started.

DD: Had you always been a movie fan and wanted to work in the film industry?

JC: Yeah, since I was about ten years old, that seems to be about the age when the idea of filmmaking becomes cool and you start using super 8 cameras. I guess now kids just whip out their phones, but back then you had to make more of an effort. My big thing was Ray Harryhausen and stop motion animation. I was shy and I was quiet, so the best thing to do when you want to make movies and are like that is to do the one frame at a time thing. Your actors are G.I. Joes and all this kind of stuff so that you don't have to go out of the house and talk to people. Come high school, I talked to one person and his name is Fred Dekker. We became pretty much best friends, we were those guys that you see in documentaries now, the guys that just did movies. Fred was super tall, I was short, I was the tech guy, he was the guy who knew actors. We blew things up, shot things, I was always doing the Harryhausen thing, I did single frame rear projection with aerial braced bats. It was kind of nuts, but we were just those guys.

HC: So, you're in California, did you end up going to film school for college?

JC: Yes, that's when the split happened as well. Fred ended up at UCLA, I ended up at USC. I got into the film program at USC, although not immediately. The film school is only a two year program so I sort of jumped into USC hoping that I would still get in and luckily I did. Fred never did, back then at UCLA they were only accepting like twenty people into the program at a time, now its like giant buildings with hundreds of people mulling about. Fred ended up becoming an English major, I would always cross town while I was doing my stuff and so we still stayed in touch.

At USC was where I got my first taste of Hollywood and the business, I wasn't in the film program yet, but I took an animation class. One day, I showed my most recent animation project to the teacher and he said, "Go to this guy and show it to him." That guy ended up being Gene Warren, who had created the effects for *The War of the Worlds*. Gene owned this company called Excelsior! which would later be called Fantasy II. I showed him what I had made and he said, "When do you want to start?" That became my summer job. Excelsior! are most famous for their work on *Land of the Lost* and later on they ended up doing the stop motion at the end of *The Terminator* and all the explosion stuff at the beginning of *Terminator 2*. Of course, I wasn't involved in any of that and I ended up animating the Pillsbury Dough Boy and the Hamburger Helper. Now it's no longer stop motion, it's all CGI so the Hamburger Helper can basically be John Wick. That's what I did during the summers while I was at USC.

When it came time for us to graduate Fred said, "Alright, come on and live with me." I go live with Fred and he's got all these other people living with him that I'm meeting, one of them was Shane Black. We had two bedrooms with four guys and there were two more guys sleeping in the living room. We called it the "Pad 'O Guys," you have to name things, you know. I was working as a gopher, a runner for Orion TV where my dad's best friend was an assistant director. Fred came out of UCLA, right out of the gate and sold a time travel script. So he's set up in the dining room with his typewriter writing the next thing, which turned out to be a 3D *Godzilla* movie for Steve Miner, none of those ever got made by the way. I'm working just to earn a living, rent was cheap at the time, and I see this ad for the very first JVC VHS recorder. It was a deck that you put on your hip and a camera that went on your shoulder. I got it and we started making videos. The editing was literally just pause, play, pause, play. Just two decks, and we figured out that you had to hit it just a second before so that you could get it to cut right. That was the "Pad 'O Guys."

Fred was the only one who was really working and we eventually moved to a bigger house when we met some other people like Ed Solomon and Chris Matheson. That's the point when Shane got a little big when he sold his script for *Lethal Weapon*. He had moved about a mile away, but he was still always there when I woke up, eating pizza, even after having made this huge sale. That's when people started making movies. Fred needed a demo reel so that he could prove that he could direct so I edited and did sound while everyone else worked on this time travel short film. We had a chem machine in the dining room, and I'm cutting film and everything. That's how he got *Night of the Creeps*. Bit of trivia, J.C., the character in *Night of the Creeps* is named after me, almost everyone calls me Jay, but Fred has always called me J.C. I should also mention that *The Simpsons* was co-created in our garage. David Silverman was one of us, he was an animator from UCLA and they were doing the little cartoon things for *The Tracy Ullman Show* that starred the Simpsons. That was all David Silverman, all planned out in our garage.

One day I picked up the phone and it was for Fred, it was his agent and he says "Do you write?" I said, "I'm trying to." He says, "OK, well, call me when you're done." I could never finish a script at that point because I am a fast typist, but an inaccurate one. I was working at Egghead Software at the time and one day I decided to quit and buy a computer. I met my future wife working at Egghead and she actually loaned me the money to buy my first computer. So basically what I did, and I do not recommend it to anybody, I quit my job and tried to be a screenwriter. Don't do that. Anyway, I wrote my first script, it was about backwards messages in music turning teenagers into suicide assassins. I had four major agencies who wanted to sign me based on that script. The script wasn't really that great but because of who I was hanging around with it was like, "Oh, are there more of you back home?" I ended up going with CAA, which ultimately was probably not the right thing for me because they dumped me after two years. I went on forty meetings, that's what CAA was great for. The thirty-eighth meeting was at this company called Taft and Barish, they had this project that I wanted to do so badly that I wrote the first ten pages for free and it got to the head of the studio, that project was *The Invaders*, the Quinn Martin TV show about alien invasion and they had the rights to it. I wrote the screenplay, it never got made, but that was my first job. I got paid guild minimum, which is huge when your rent is five hundred dollars a month, and I got into the Writer's Guild. That was the beginning of my writing career.

Around that time, everyone started working for Joel Silver. Fred had a script called *Ricochet*, that ended up being made, Shane was doing *Lethal Weapon 2,* my friend Robert Reneau did *Action Jackson*. I get called in to do the pitch for *The Adventures of Ford Fairlane*, it wasn't really totally my thing so I asked my roommate Dave Arnott if he wanted to write it with me. And then in March of 1988, the longest writer's strike in history happens. One hundred fifty-four days. Of course you can write your own stuff during the strike, but you really can't do anything else. We got out of the writer's strike and there was this show, *Freddy's Nightmares* that was hiring anyone who had ever directed horror. They contacted Fred and he said, "OK sure, I'll do that, but I want my friend to write it." Fred was going to develop the story with me and have me write the script. It was originally titled "Accidents do Happen," that's why Freddy says it at the end of the episode. If you ever get to see any of the scripts you'll notice that they were constantly changing the titles. So, the first half was gonna be a time travel thing, and we both loved *War Games*, so the second half we just tried to figure out how to put ourselves in a missile silo. That was the draw of doing an anthology show, you could basically do whatever you want as long as its super cheap. Fred ended up not being able to do the show due to another commitment. The producers saw the script and said, "We're gonna do this one next," and Jonathan Betuel ended up directing. Since they wanted to do the episode right away, pretty much everything you see on the show is how it was written. Typically the norm is that the producers will put your script through the writing staff for re-writes, which is how TV is supposed to work. So that was it, I was about to get my first produced show.

The producers invited me out to the set, which like much TV at the time, was just a warehouse out in the Valley. I park and walk in to the set and I turn a corner and there is George Lazenby sitting at a desk and I was instantly brought back to when I was ten years old sitting in the theater watching him play James Bond in *On Her Majesty's Secret Service*, I was gobsmacked. I'm still pretty quiet at the time so I just sit back and watch George Lazenby act for half a day. Then they broke for lunch, lunch was, I remember this well, bologna sandwiches. Now, I had been on the set of *Die Hard* at this point and Joel Silver is famous for catering lobster and steak and giant tubs of ice cream, but *Freddy's Nightmares*, here's a bologna sandwich, which I hadn't had since I was five or whatever. Still though, great people and I was very happy to be there. The second half of the day I turn a corner and there's a nuclear missile silo hallway, a big panel of buttons and everything. Essentially that was my first day of production for something that I had written, it was really really cool.

HC: When you were brought on to write the episode were you given any guidelines? I know that it had that weird "A" story, "B" story split in the middle.

JC: Yes, Jeff Freilich, the person who actually created that concept, with Gil Adler of course, because the producers wanted to be able to syndicate it in two halves so that they had forty-four episodes to be able to sell. In those days, you're always behind in television, TV shows now are eight, ten episodes, we had to make twenty-two or twenty-four and it was constant. It's a little bit better with syndication since you're selling it as a package, it's worse with the network when the show has to go air tomorrow. That's one of the reasons why they jumped on my script so quickly, because it was formatted, and it worked and it was simple. I didn't get the full rundown, no one said, "Do this, do this, do this," it really was just what Fred and I wanted to do, a time travel show and a *War Games* show. That leads us into my second episode which was my true initiation into *Freddy's Nightmares*. Jonathan Betuel loved me, he said, "Let's do another one." So I sit down with my notepad with Jon and things get wackier and wackier. There was no bible, most TV shows have a bible that's essentially the style of the show. It's all verbal on *Freddy's Nightmares*. The second half of the episode, way before my time, I wanted to do *Inception*-style how many times can we have a dream within a dream within a dream. It was a different experience for me than the first time to write this crazy Freddy thing. So, I got to go on another set and I got to watch Dick Miller be Dick Miller. And just to wrap all this around, it wasn't until after all of this that *The Adventures of Ford Fairlane* was made. The casting was changed from Bruce Willis to Andrew Dice Clay because Willis wanted to do *Hudson Hawk* and the studio though that Clay was going to be the next Eddie Murphy. The script doesn't read like a Clay movie so in typical Hollywood tradition, we were fired. It's not fired, you just don't get hired back, so they hired the hot screenwriter at the time, Dan Waters, he had just done *Heathers* and was going to do *Batman Returns,* to do the rewrite.

After *The Adventures of Ford Fairlane,* Jeff Freilich calls me up and says, "Do you and Dave want to write something for Lorimar?" For Lorimar we wrote a pilot for *Justice League of America*, because Lorimar was owned by Warner Brothers, who owned DC. We weren't allowed to use anybody like Superman or Batman, so we're doing Blue Beetle and Fire & Ice. It would have been ridiculous, we had Martian Manhunter grabbing missiles from the sky and Doctor Fate sucking in nuclear explosions into his helmet. This was 1991, what were the effects going to look like on TV? It would have been like that Roger Corman *Fantastic Four* movie. Needless to say, it never got made. One day Michael DeLuca called me up and asked if I wanted to be involved with a *Nightmare on Elm Street* movie, which would have been part six. Right from the beginning they told me that they were doing parallel scripts and they were going to choose which one they wanted to make. So I write *Nightmare on Elm Street 6* really quickly and it was pretty ridiculous. The script was based on a comic book and the opening action sequence would have been more expensive than all of the other movies put together. DeLuca got the script and said, "This is the best first draft of anything we have ever gotten, but we are gonna go with Rachel's script." Basically after that, for like six years, I worked with Jeff Freilich on *Dark Justice*. *Dark Justice* was the Friday night show on CBS's "Crimetime after Primetime." We shot the first season in Barcelona but then moved to a warehouse in Chatsworth once the Barcelona money dried up. The show was moving super fast and that was the point where I put my hand up and asked if I could direct. Freilich agreed and ultimately that show is what got me into the DGA.

I kept working in TV after that, the next show was *Poltergeist: The Legacy.* That show was wild because it had nothing to do with the movies. I was a freelancer and did six episodes of that show. *Poltergeist* would air first on Showtime with nude scenes, so those ended up being my first sex scenes that were produced, and then it would air cut down in syndication like a month later. *Mortal Kombat: Conquest* was a hoot, we just did that out of a guy's house in Toluca Lake because the show was shooting in Florida. It was all syndicated television, the big downside of syndicated is that you don't get in the mix, you don't get on network lists. My agents were doing a good job getting me these smaller gigs and stuff, but when it started to slow down a bit I went back into features. My advice is, never say no to anything. I made a few mistakes saying no, I was tired at the end of *Dark Justice* and I wanted to get back into features. I was still using the script for The Invaders as a sample and one day my agent calls and says, "There's this thing about UFOs." I said no because I wanted to work on directing and stuff so they didn't send me out for it. It was *The X-Files.*

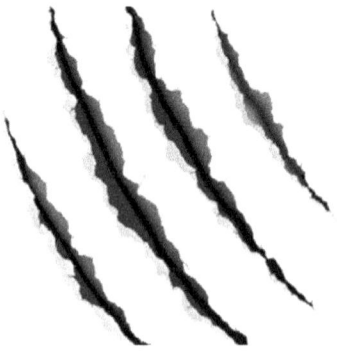

KEN WIEDERHORN

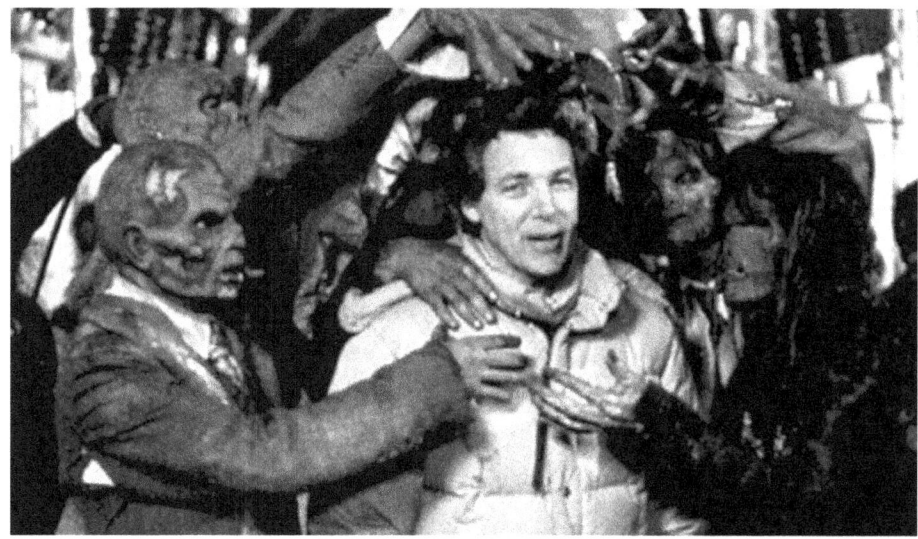

Ken Wiederhorn is an American film and television producer, writer and director. Wiederhorn holds a Master of Fine Arts degree in film/ cinema/ video studies from Columbia University in New York.[22] His thesis film, *Manhattan Melody* was the winner of the Motion Picture Academy Student Film Award for best drama. After Columbia University, Wiederhorn went to work for CBS as an editor for the news and documentary unit.[23]

Shortly thereafter a film school colleague, Ruben Trane contacted Wiederhorn about a feature film opportunity. Trane had managed to raise a couple hundred thousand dollars to make a feature, the catch was that the financiers wanted a horror picture. Trane asked Wiederhorn to come to Florida to collaborate on the project, which would become the intensely atmospheric film, *Shock Waves*, the first feature in a new sub-genre: the underwater Nazi zombie movie. The film starred Robert Carradine and Peter Cushing; Wiederhorn would direct the picture, while Trane would produce and photograph, with principal photography beginning in July, 1975 under the title, *Death Corps*. The film was shot on 16mm, in and around Miami Florida and also utilized a shipwrecked vessel, the SS Sapona, located off the coast of the island of Bimini in the Bahamas. While largely unsuccessful during it's initial release, the film gained cult notoriety on home video and DVD many years later.

After the film, Wiederhorn went back to work for CBS. Several years later, the CBS Television Network acquired *Shock Waves* for a late night TV time slot.

Wiederhorn had never mentioned the film to his coworkers, who were quite surprised to find out that he had directed a horror film. After meeting with some associates at CBS, it began to become clear to Wiederhorn that the film was going to be a problem for him and his career as a documentary filmmaker.[24]

It was around this time that he received a call from a low budget producer who had seen *Shock Waves* asking if he would be interested in directing another feature, this time a comedy film. Because of the strained working relationship he now had with CBS, he agreed. The 1979 film, *King Frat*, a bad *Animal House* knock off became his second feature film. His next feature was 1981's *Eyes of a Stranger*, an early entry in the post-*Friday the 13th* slasher boom. The producers of *Eyes of the Stranger* were told by Paramount Pictures that if the movie was bloody, they would distribute it. Tom Savini was brought in by the producers to create the necessary gore, although Wiederhorn states that his job was really to hold Savini back. Warner Brothers ended up offering more money than Paramount, but ultimately mishandled the release of the film and it went largely unnoticed.

Wiederhorn would then relocate from New York to Los Angeles and was soon after offered a goofy kid's comedy with *E.T.* undertones called, *Call Me Meathead*. The movie was made for a few million dollars, his highest budget to date, and TriStar Pictures took the completed film and retitled it *Meatballs II* to capitalize on the success of the hit film *Meatballs*, for which they had obtained the sequel rights.

Wiederhorn began to focus on writing and penned a horror comedy about a kid who has a run in with a bunch of zombies. In another instance of a producer having sequel rights to a hit movie, his film was retitled *Return of the Living Dead II*. Wiederhorn was hesitant to proceed after the mishandling and retitling of his previous film, but after receiving encouragement from *Return of the Living Dead* writer/ director Dan O'Bannon, he moved forward with making the sequel. *Return of the Living Dead II* opened on about twelve hundred screens, but once again didn't really find it's audience until home video.

After *Return of the Living Dead II*, Wiederhorn made the jump to directing television and landed a gig on *Freddy's Nightmares*. Over the two seasons of the show he would direct seven episodes, more than any other director involved in the series. Wiederhorn would go on to direct two episodes of *21 Jump Street* before returning to work with producer Jeff Freilich, directing six episodes of *Dark Justice*. His next, and final, feature film was 1993's *A House in the Hills* starring Michael Madsen. *A House in the Hills* would also reunite him with *Shock Waves* and *Eyes of a Stranger* composer, Richard Einhorn. Wiederhorn would soon after return to New York to work on television documentaries before eventually retiring from the entertainment industry.

KEVIN YAGHER

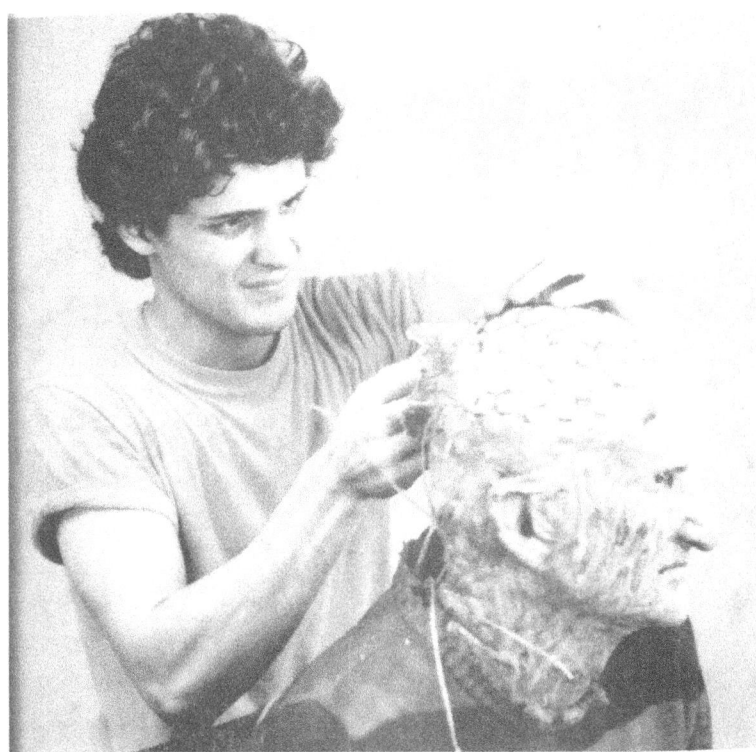

Kevin Yagher is a special effects artist who is known for his work on the *Bill and Ted* franchise, *Trick or Treat, 976-EVIL, Face/Off, Hellraiser: Bloodlines* (which he also directed), *Starship Troopers, Mission Impossible 2* and many others. For over 30 years his company, Kevin Yagher Productions Inc, has been a leader in special effects for the film industry. Yagher is most famous for creating the Chucky doll from the *Child's Play* films. Shortly after his work on *Child's Play*, Yagher was approached by HBO to design the Cryptkeeper character for their series *Tales from the Crypt*. Kevin also directed the wraparound sequences and several promotional spots for the show, one of which earned him an Emmy award.[25]

In addition to Chucky and the Cryptkeeper, Yagher also had a hand in one of horror's most notable icons, Freddy Krueger, designing the makeup for *Nightmare on Elm St. 2, 3* and *4*, and he was the lead Freddy makeup designer for 22 episodes of *Freddy's Nightmares* from 1988-1989.

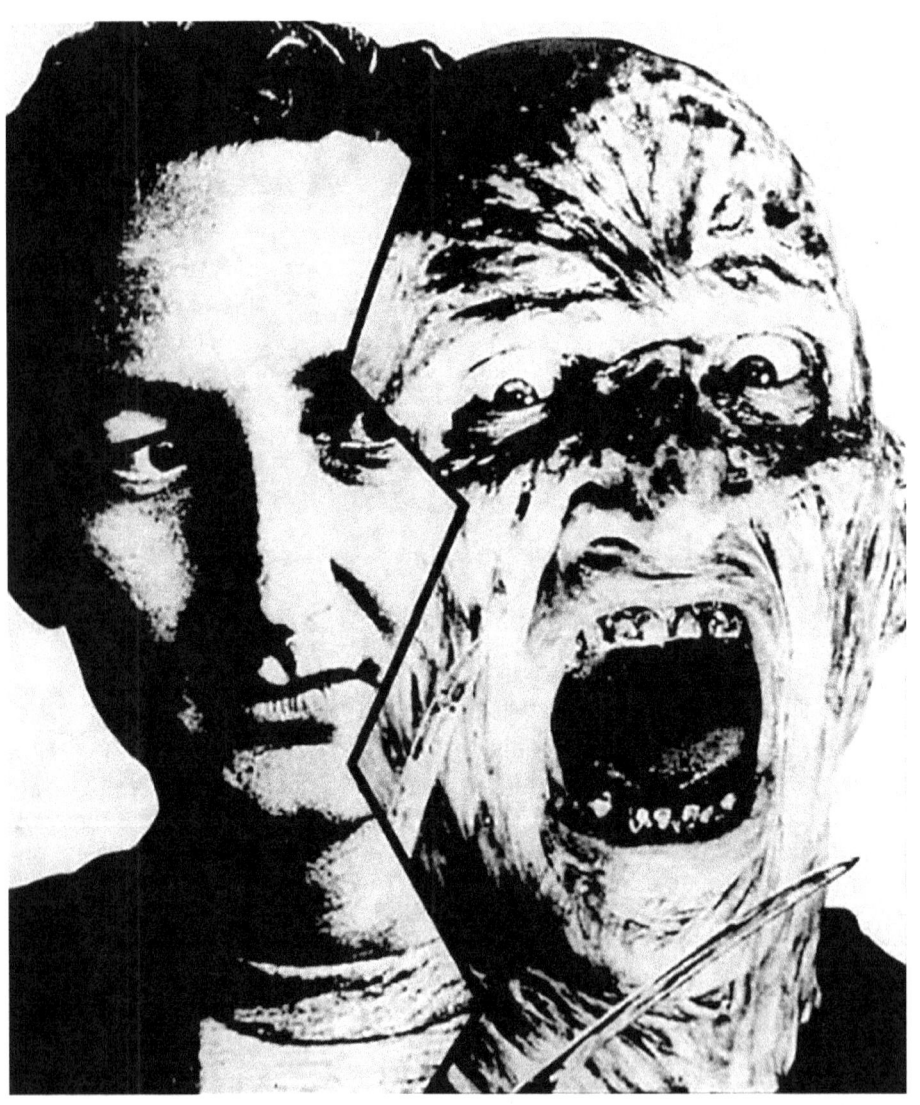

ROBERT ENGLUND

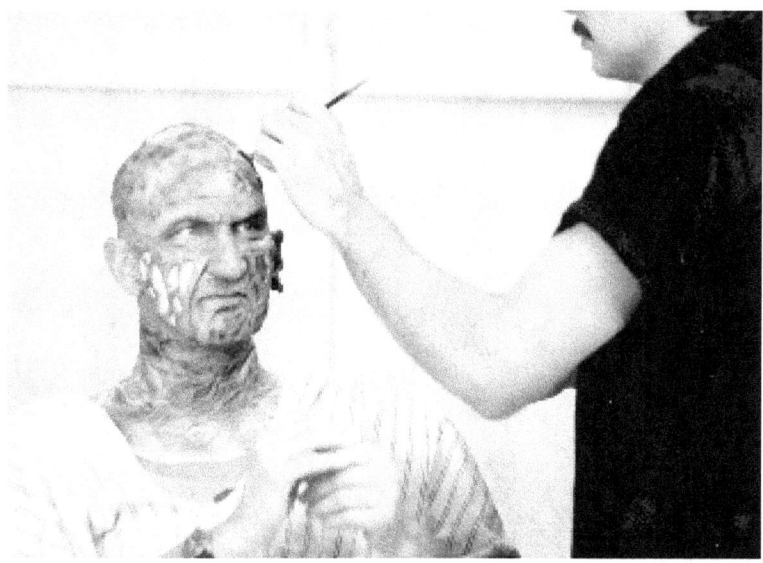

Robert Englund is an American actor and director best known for his portrayal of child murderer and dream demon, Freddy Krueger, in the *Nightmare on Elm Street* franchise. Englund was born in Glendale, California and trained to be an actor at the California State University, Northridge, Royal Academy of Dramatic Art.[26] Englund had five successful years on stage performing in regional theater before returning home to the West Coast in search of film work.[27]

His first feature film role was the character Whitey in Daniel Petrie's 1974 neo-noir crime film, *Buster and Billie*. In 1976, Englund would appear in Tobe Hooper's follow up to *The Texas Chainsaw Massacre, Eaten Alive*. Englund also had roles in the 1981 films *Dead & Buried* and *Galaxy of Terror*, directed by Gary Sherman and Bruce D. Clark, respectively; the latter being produced by Roger Corman's New World Pictures.

During this time, Englund also had a successful run in episodic television and made for TV movies, most notably his recurring role of Willie in the series *V.* His breakout performance came in 1984 when he first donned the Freddy Krueger makeup in Wes Craven's supernatural horror film *A Nightmare on Elm Street*. Englund instantly became a horror icon and launched a franchise which would see him play the character in eight films and two seasons of the television series *Freddy's Nightmares*, often spending four or more hours per day in make up.

Englund made his directorial debut with the 1988 film *976-EVIL*. He would also direct two episodes of *Freddy's Nightmares*, "Cabin Fever" and Monkey Dreams." The opportunity to direct was a significant part of his deal to return as Krueger for the series and also helped him to get into the DGA. Over the years that followed, Englund has amassed more than one hundred film and television credits. Englund also hosted the *Horror Hall of Fame* awards show three times from 1990 until 1992.[28]

Some of his other more notable film works include:
The Phantom of the Opera (1989)
The Adventures of Ford Fairlane (1990)
The Mangler (1995)
Wishmaster (1997)
Urban Legend (1998)
Strangeland (1998)
2001 Maniacs (2005)
Hatchet (2006)
Behind the Mask: The Rise of Leslie Vernon (2006)
Zombie Strippers (2008)

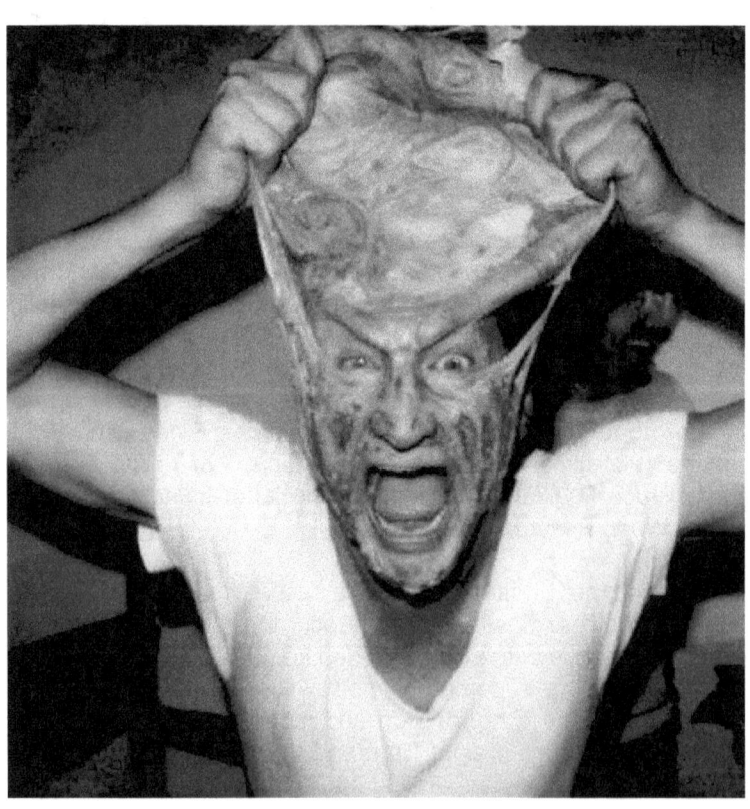

SPRINGWOOD

HIGH SCHOOL

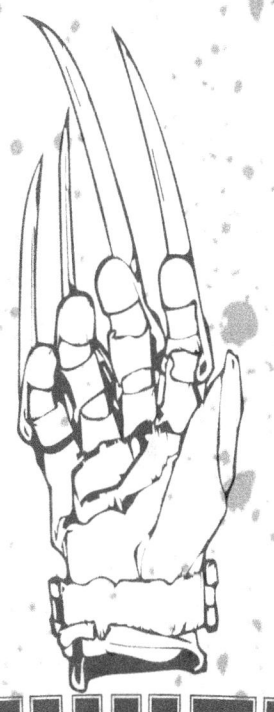

ACTIVITIES

1988-1990

SPRINGWOOD HIGH

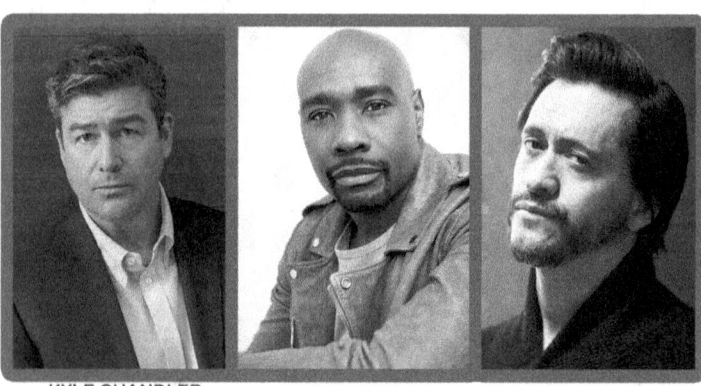

KYLE CHANDLER
S02E05

MORRIS CHESTNUT
S02E19

CLIFTON COLLINS JR.
S02E16

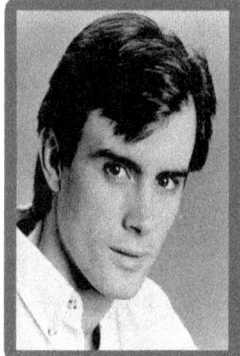
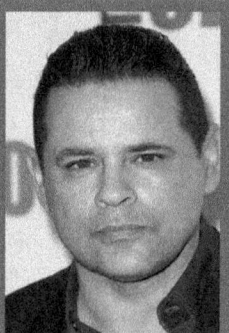
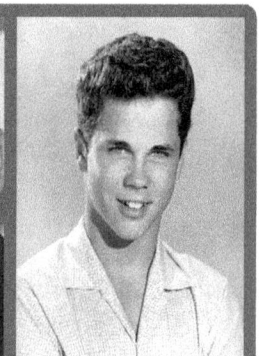

JEFFREY COMBS
S01E17

RAYMOND CRUZ
S02E22

TONY DOW
S02E15
S02E20

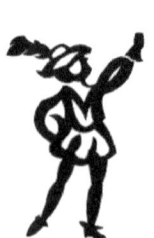
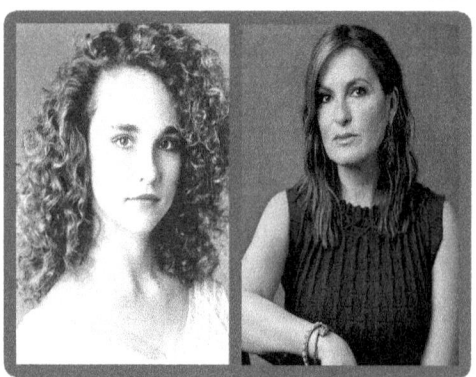
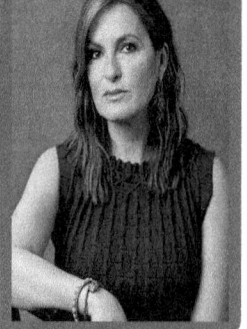

DIANE FRANKLIN
S01E10

MARISKA HARGITAY
S01E04

DRAMA CLUB

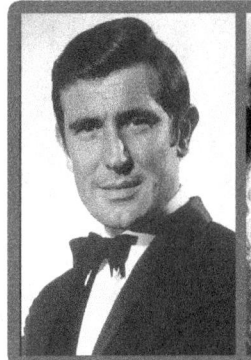
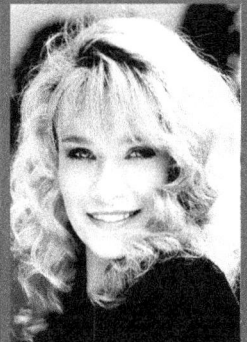
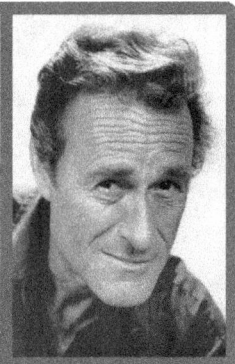

GEORGE LAZENBY
S01E12

LAR PARK LINCOLN
S01E02

DICK MILLER
S01E20

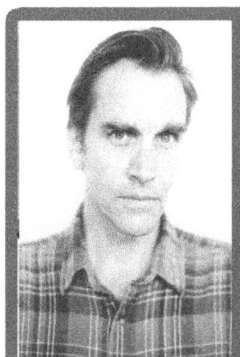
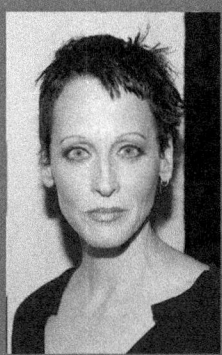
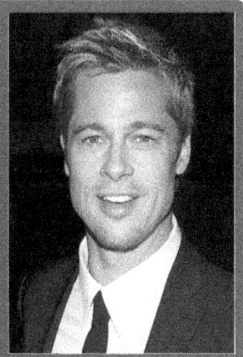

BILL MOSELEY
S01E14

LORI PETTY
S01E03

BRAD PITT
S01E14

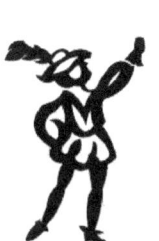
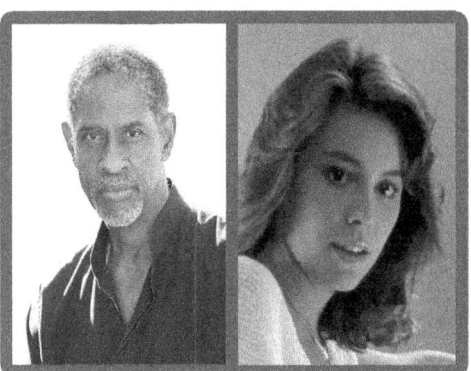

TIM RUSS
S02E20

JILL WHITLOW
S01E08

SPRINGWOOD HIGH

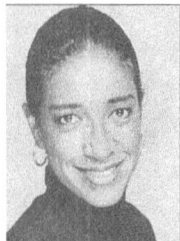

ANITA W. ADDISON
S02E22

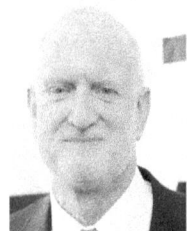

GILBERT ADLER
S02E18

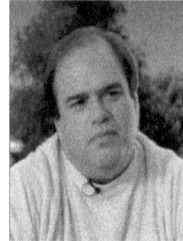

JONATHAN BETUEL
S01E12, S01E20

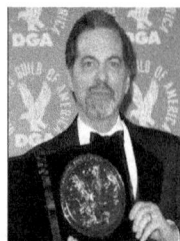

CHUCK BRAVERMAN
S02E07

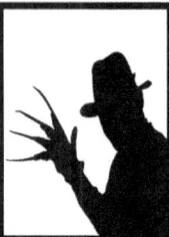

DAVID K. CALLOWAY
S01E21, S02E15

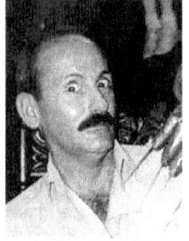

TOM DeSIMONE
S01E05, S02E04, S02E11,
S02E12

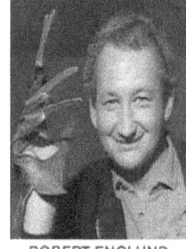

ROBERT ENGLUND
S01E16, S02E09

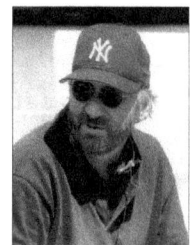

JEFF FREILICH
S01E19

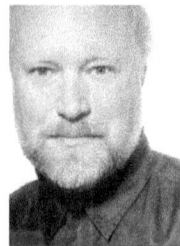

BILL FROELICH
S02E10

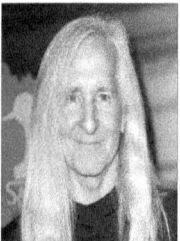

MICK GARRIS
S01E03

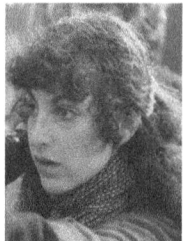

LISA GOTTLIEB
S01E06

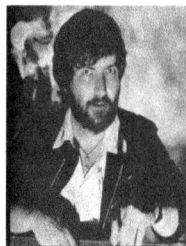

TOBE HOOPER
S01E01

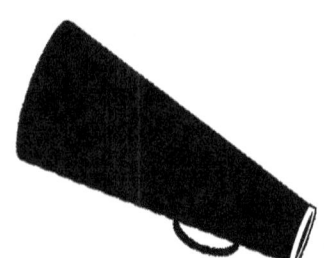

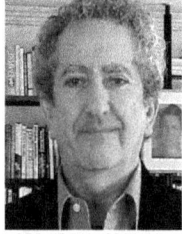

GEORGE KACZENDER
S01E10, S01E14, S02E01

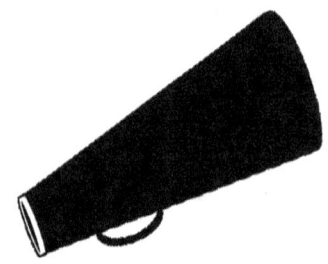

DIRECTORS CLUB

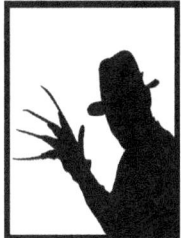

MICHAEL KLIEN
S01E15

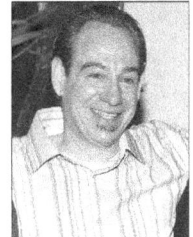

JOHN LAFIA
S01E09, S01E17

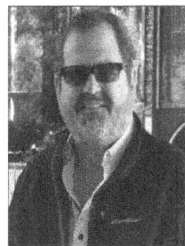

MICHAEL LANGE
S01E08, S01E13

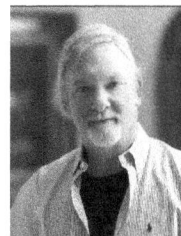

DWIGHT LITTLE
S01E11

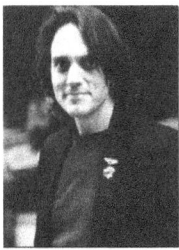

WILLIAM MALONE
S02E02, S02E06, S02E14

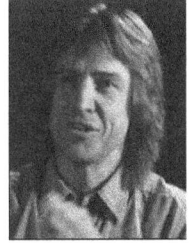

TOM McLOUGHLIN
S01E02

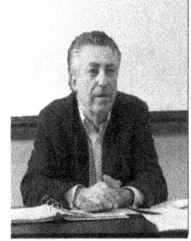

JERRY OLSON
S01E22

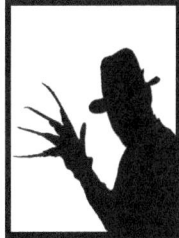

JAMES QUINN
S02E08

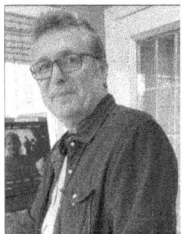

KEITH SAMPLES
S02E19

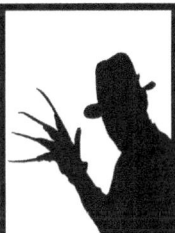

RICHARD T. SCHOR
S02E21

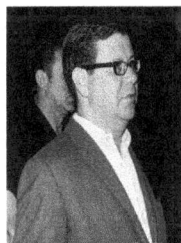

DON WEIS
S02E05

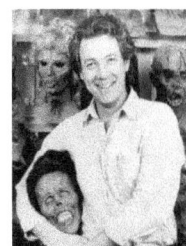

KEN WIEDERHORN
S01E04, S01E07, S01E18,
S02E03, S02E13, S02E16,
S02E17

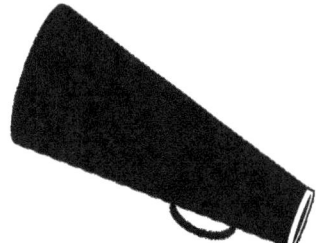

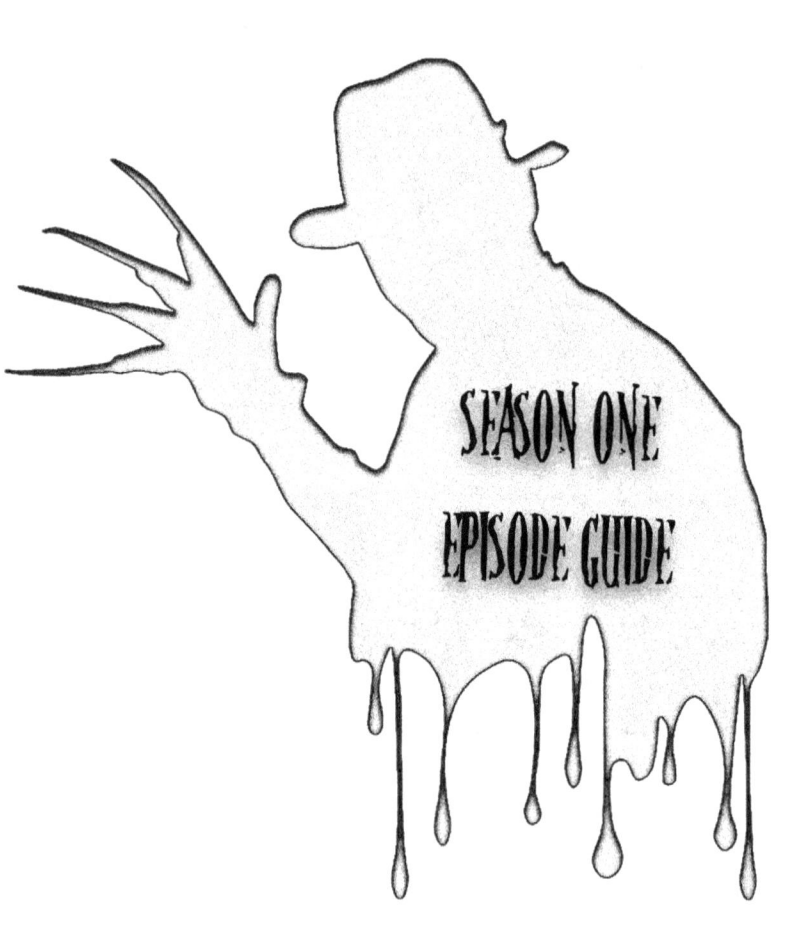

SEASON ONE

EPISODE GUIDE

"No More Mr. Nice Guy"

Original Air Date: Sunday, October 9, 1988
Season 1, Episode 1

Director: Tobe Hooper

Writers: Rhet Topham, Michael DeLuca, David Erhman

Cast: Robert Englund, Ian Patrick Williams, Anne E. Curry, Mark Herrier, William Frankfather, Alba Francesca, Tyde Kierney, Gry Park, Hili Park, Gwen E. Davis, Tamara Souza, Robert Goen, Steven D. Reisch

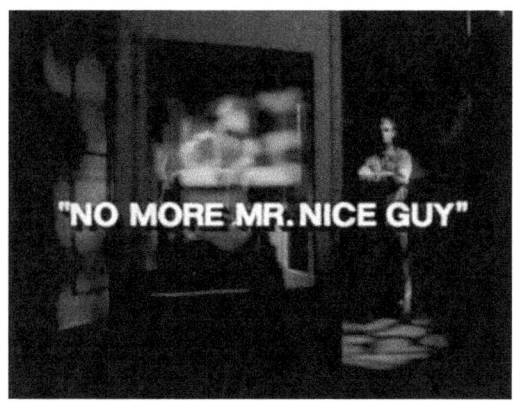

Synopsis

Dream haunting serial killer Freddy Krueger's origin story. Lt. Blocker, a Springwood police officer catches Freddy attempting to kill his daughters and arrests him. During Krueger's trial it is revealed that he was never read his Miranda Rights at the time of his arrest, and thus, must be released. The parents of Springwood form a lynch mob and catch Krueger, planning to kill him. The plot is interrupted by Lt. Blocker, who becomes the reluctant executioner, dousing Krueger in gasoline and setting him ablaze. Believing that justice had finally been served, the townspeople attempt to return to normal, but soon find that Freddy is anything but dead.

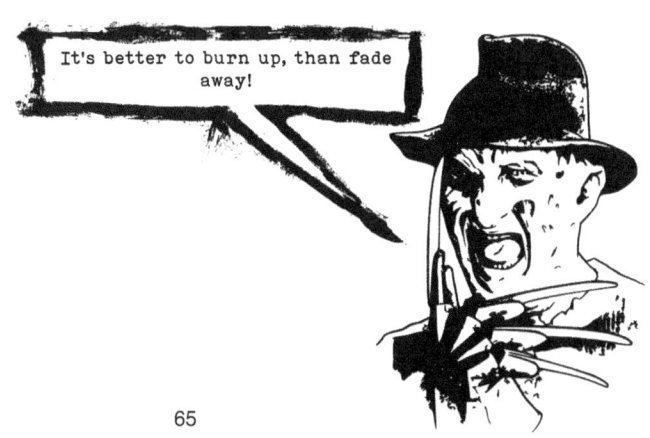

It's better to burn up, than fade away!

"It's a Miserable Life"

Original Air Date: Sunday, October 16, 1988
Season 1, Episode 2

Director: Tom McLoughlin

Writers: Michael DeLuca, Paul Rosselli

Cast: Lar Park Lincoln, John Cameron Mitchell, Burr DeBenning, Peter Iacangelo, Nancy McLoughlin, Annie O'Donnell, Tracy Shakespear, Michael Melvin, Kyle Scott Jackson, Adam Karien, Robert Englund

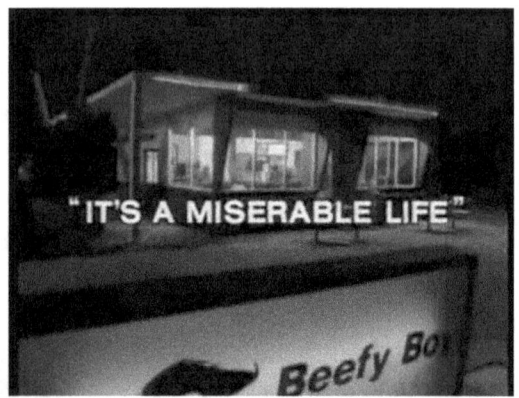

Synopsis

A Story - Beefy Boy fast food restaurant worker Brian becomes the victim of a drive-by shooter and a moment becomes a lifetime as his miserable life flashes before his eyes.

B Story - Meanwhile, Karen, Brian's girlfriend is also shot by the same assassin and is forced to live out her paralyzing fear of hospitals as she is tormented by hospital staff and visions of her dead boyfriend.

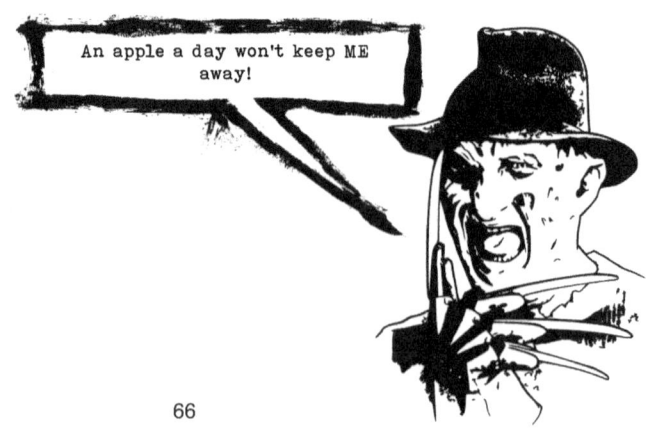

"Killer Instinct"

Original Air Date: Sunday, October 23, 1988
Season 1, Episode 3

Director: Mick Garris

Writer: Alan B. Ury

Cast: Yvette Nipar, Lori Petty, Kane Picoy, Lee Kessler, Anthony Barton, Stephen R. Franken, Daniel T. Trent, Claire C. Peck, Gregory C. Wilkinson, L.E. Mosko, Frederick Long, V.C. Dupree, Robert Englund

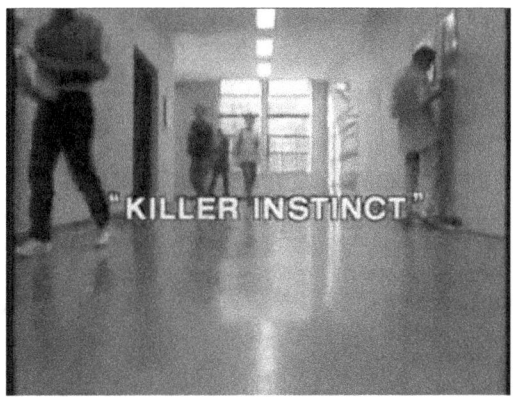

Synopsis

A Story - High school track star Christina has lost her edge and is kicked off the team. Christina is given an heirloom charm with magical powers that once belonged to her mother. She uses the talisman to help herself and to hurt Nikki, her rival on the field who also tried to steal her boyfriend.

B Story - Nikki steals the talisman and accidentally kills Christina by using it. Haunted by the ghost of Christina, Nikki is driven insane.

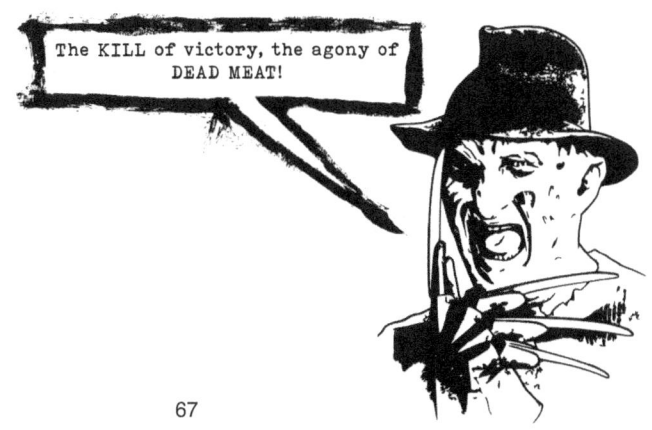

The KILL of victory, the agony of DEAD MEAT!

"Freddy's Tricks and Treats"

Original Air Date: Sunday, October 30, 1988
Season 1, Episode 4

Director: Ken Wiederhorn

Writers: Alan L. Katz, Gil Adler

Cast: Mariska Hargitay, Darren Dalton, Daniel McDonald, Cameron Thor, Elsa Raven, Chuck Sloan, Don Maxwell, Shiri Appleby, Anthony Palermo, Robin Lynn Heath, Robert Englund

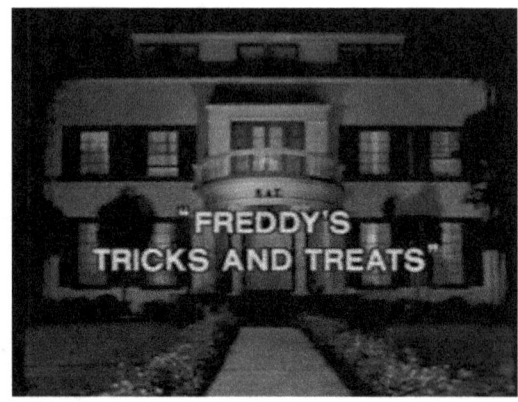

Synopsis

A Story - It's Halloween in Springwood. Deciding to study instead of partaking in the Halloween festivities, a sexually repressed medical student, Marsha, is tormented by none other than Freddy himself.

B Story - Zach attempts to record Marsha's dreams on video, but instead of trying to help her, he's out to exploit her by conducting his experiment on her in Freddy's boiler room. Zach's professor pulls the plug on his research, but the two youths continue on regardless, with dire consequences.

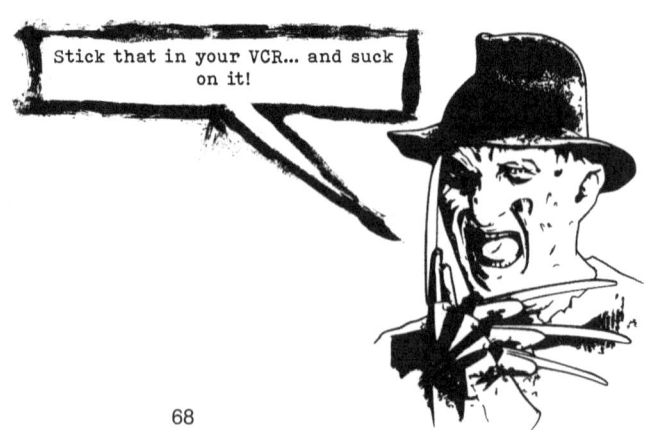

Stick that in your VCR... and suck on it!

"Judy Miller, Come on Down"

Original Air Date: Sunday, November 6, 1988
Season 1, Episode 5

Director: Tom DeSimone

Writers: Jack Temchin, Michael DeLuca

Cast: Siobhan E. McCafferty, John Demita, Susan Oliver, Larry Anderson, Georgia Dell, Charles C. Stevenson Jr., Theresa Ring, Peggy Mannix, Jim Landis, Robert Englund

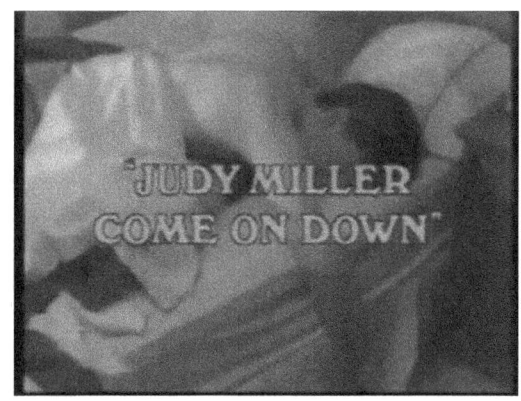

Synopsis

A Story - Judy Miller is a game show fanatic, and the sole breadwinner in a home with a law student husband and overbearing in-laws. She becomes a contestant on a show with dark consequences: if she wins, the prize is one million dollars, but it will also cost her dearly.

B Story - A now wealthy Judy is visited by a strange woman who claims to be her from the future. The woman tries to impart on Judy the grave importance of letting the fortune go before it's too late.

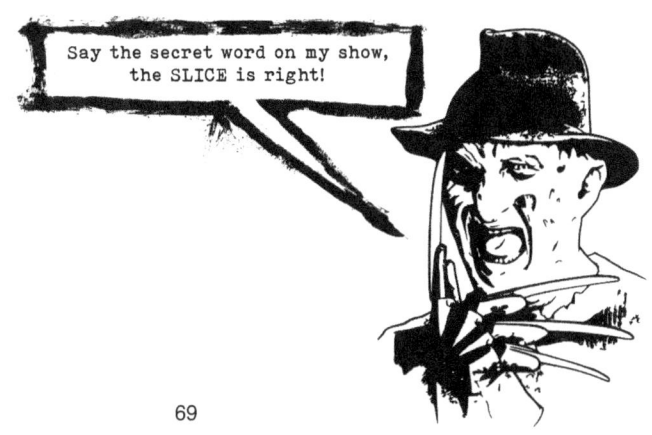

Say the secret word on my show, the SLICE is right!

"Saturday Night Special"

Original Air Date: Sunday, November 13, 1988
Season 1, Episode 6

Director: Lisa Gottlieb

Writers: Don Bohlinger, James Nathan

Cast: Shari Shattuck, Scott Burkholder, Paul Lieber, Joyce Hyser, Molly Kleator, Robert Lesser, Jerry Colker, Robert Englund

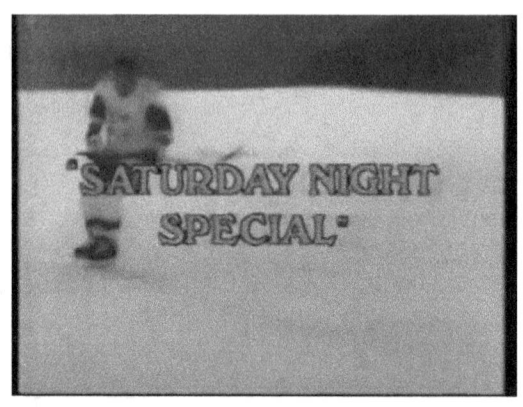

Synopsis

A Story - Gordon wants a beautiful woman. After making a tape filled with lies for a video dating service, he scores a date with Lana, the woman of his dreams. Gordon's lies soon catch up with him as Lana sees right through him.

B Story - Lana's sister, Mary, is unhappy with her appearance and is convinced by Lana to get plastic surgery. Mary soon learns that beauty is only skin deep when things begin to take a turn.

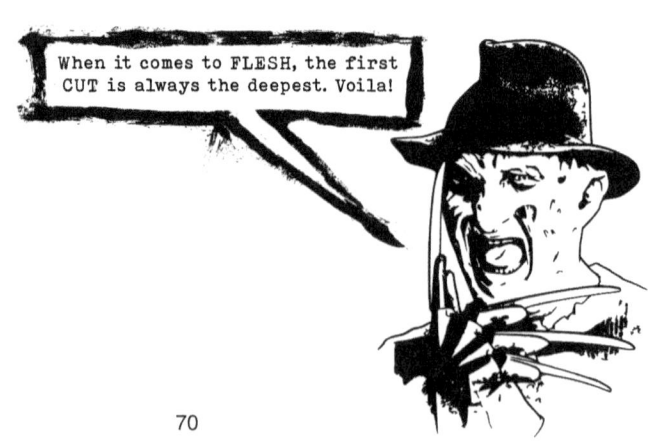

When it comes to FLESH, the first CUT is always the deepest. Voila!

"Sister's Keeper"

Original Air Date: Sunday, November 20, 1988
Season 1, Episode 7

Director: Ken Wiederhorn

Writers: Michael DeLuca, Jeff Freilich

Cast: Hili Park, Gry Park, Anne E.
Curry, Joshua Cox, Chip Hipkins,
Jeff Bennett, Robin Antin, Robert
Englund

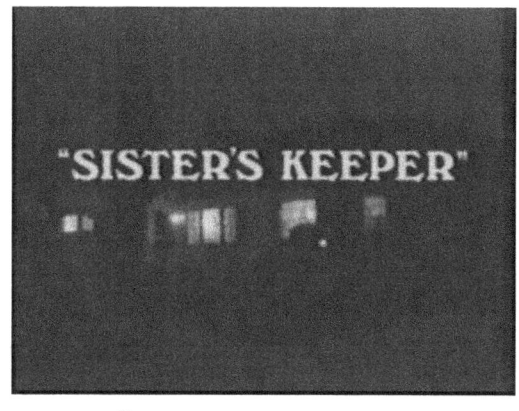

Synopsis

Lt. Blocker's twin daughters are back in this follow up to the season opener "No More Mr. Nice Guy." Freddy terrorizes Merit in her dreams and her sister Lisa experiences the real life effects. Lisa finally begins to believe Merit that Freddy is real and is after them. The two teens hatch a plan to to into their dreams together to stop Krueger but things don't go exactly as planned.

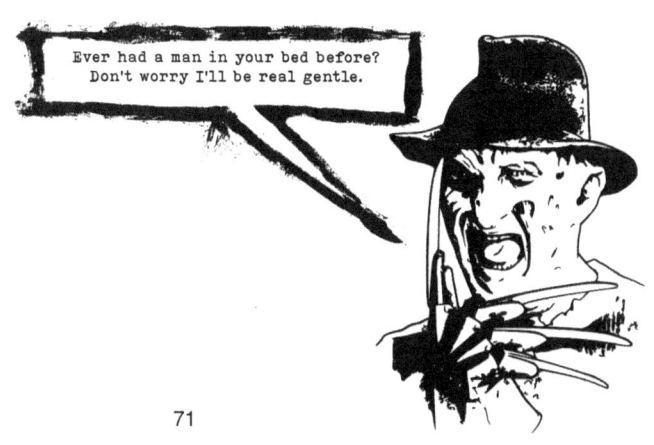

"Mother's Day"

Original Air Date: Sunday, November 27, 1988
Season 1, Episode 8

Director: Michael Lange

Writer: David Ehrman

Cast: Elizabeth Savage, Jill Whitlow, Byron Thames, Judith Baldwin, Byron Morrow, Arell Blanton, Paul Ben-Victor, Clyde R. Jones, Antoni Stutz, Geoffrey Forward, Gwen E. Davis, Patrick Sherick, Robert Englund

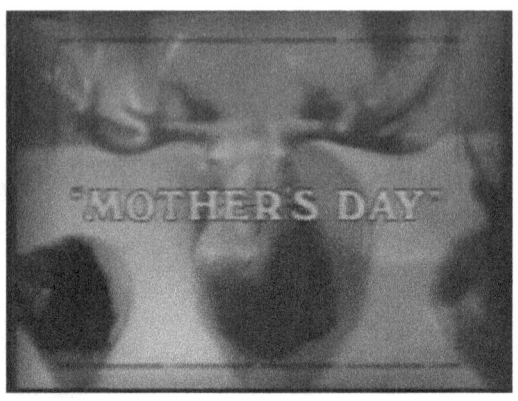

Synopsis

A Story - Billy has just moved into the old Elm St. house with his mother and abusive stepfather. When his parents go out of town Billy meets the neighbor girl, Barbara. Barbara convinces him to host a party and the guests turn out to be an absolute nightmare.

B Story - Barbara's mother is a late night radio DJ who is so entangled with her career that she neglects her teenage daughter. A caller on her show threatens to kill his landlord and the host eggs him on, becoming an accessory to murder.

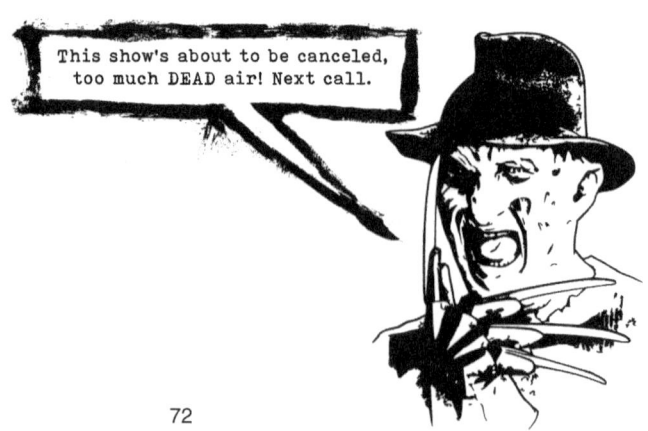

This show's about to be canceled, too much DEAD air! Next call.

"Rebel Without a Car"

Original Air Date: Sunday, December 11, 1988
Season 1, Episode 9

Director: John Lafia

Writer: Christopher Trumbo

Cast: Katie Barberi, Craig Hurley, Denise Loveday, Diana Barrows, Chris Ufland, G. Adam Gifford, Margaret Howell, Ria Pavia, Michele Scipp, Richard Campus, Kevin J. Redzinski, Robert Englund

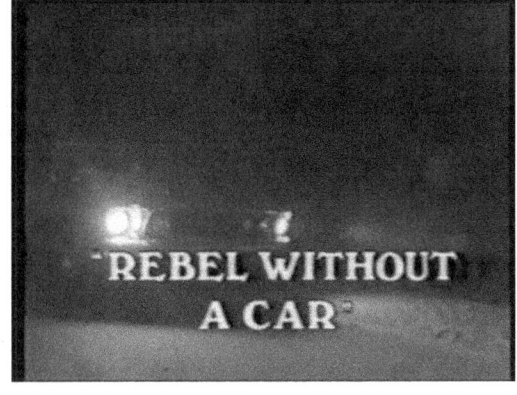

Synopsis

A Story - Alex, an employee at the Beefy Boy fast food restaurant, just wants out of Springwood. When he comes across an abandoned muscle car Alex thinks he has found his ticket to freedom, but the car's deceased former owner isn't going to let him out of Springwood that easily.

B Story - Alex's girlfriend, Connie, is desperate to get into the Omega Kappa Pi sorority. When the hazing goes too far Connie turns the tables on the sisters and gives them a taste of their own medicine.

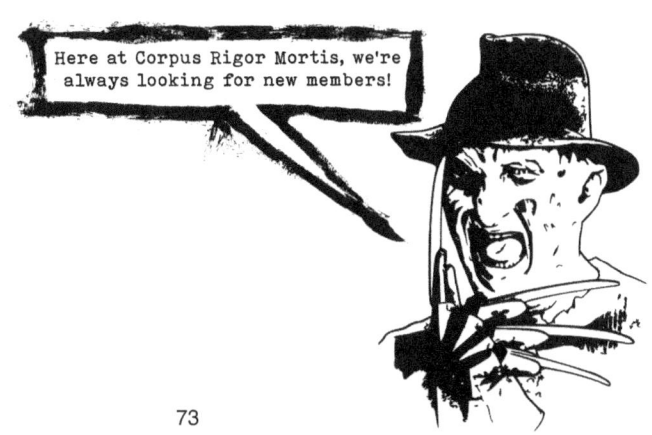

Here at Corpus Rigor Mortis, we're always looking for new members!

73

"The Bride Wore Red"

Original Air Date: Sunday, December 18, 1988
Season 1, Episode 10

Director: George Kaczender

Writer: Howard Lakin

Cast: Diane Franklin, Eddie Driscoll, Katherine Moffat, Gary Wood, Arthur David Roberts, Jamie P. Gomez, Margaret Shinn, Michele Pawk, Susan Singer, Katy Walker, Jake Jacobs, Robert Englund

Synopsis

A Story - Gavin and Jessica are about to tie the knot. Gavin attempts to assuage Jessica's fears of his commitment, but a mysterious stripper that he meets at his bachelor party may have other plans for him.

B Story - A traumatic memory of her father's infidelity weighs on newlywed Jessica. Angered by her suspicions about Gavin and this painful memory, Jessica attempts to expose the adulterous nature of the men of Springwood.

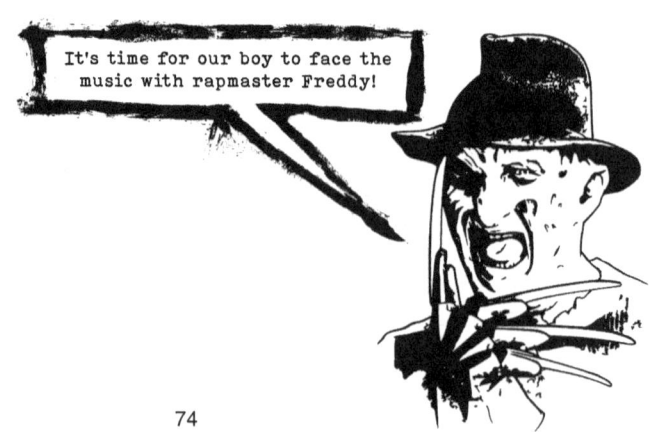

It's time for our boy to face the music with rapmaster Freddy!

"Do Dreams Bleed"

Original Air Date: Sunday, January 8, 1989
Season 1, Episode 11

Director: Dwight Little

Writer: Michael DeLuca

Cast: Damon Martin, Sarah G. Buxton, Jeff McCarthy, Gloria Carlin, Arlette Stella Poland, Joe Faust, Cesca Lawrence, Meshell Dillon, Michael James, Robert Englund

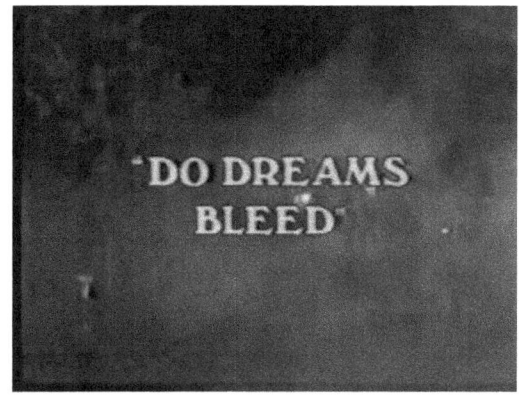

Synopsis

A Story - Springwood High football star, John, is having nightmares after discovering the body of "The Springwood Chopper's" latest victim. He learns more about the killer with each dream, but can he handle the truth about The Chopper's true identity?

B-Story - John has been committed after being identified as "The Springwood Chopper." His girlfriend, Roni, beings to suffer from the same dreams as she attempts to clear her boyfriend's name.

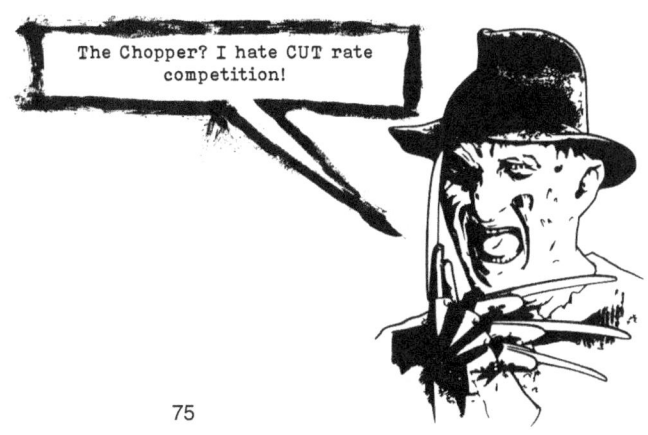

The Chopper? I hate CUT rate competition!

"The End of the World"

Original Air Date: Sunday, January 15, 1989
Season 1, Episode 12

Director: Jonathan Betuel

Writer: James Cappe

Cast: Terri Semper, Gloria Loring, Jack Manning, Mary Kohnert, George Lazenby, Andrew Prine, Walter Gotell, Albert Hall, Robert Englund

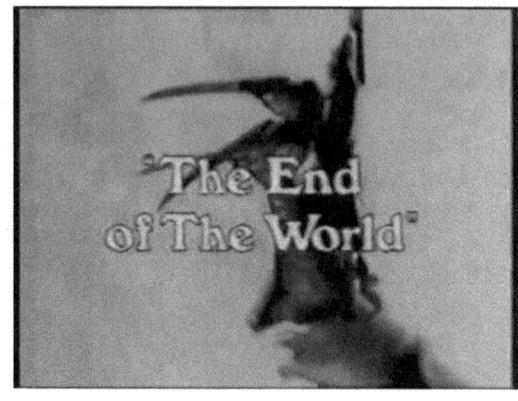

Synopsis

A Story - Amy is having a recurring dream from her past and she discovers that if she changes things in the dream, they become real in the present. While she is able to right some wrongs, she soon learns a hard truth: some things are inevitable, especially in Springwood.

B Story - Amy's dream abilities get the attention of the CIA when it's revealed that she was able to obtain nuclear launch codes from within her dream. The agency attempts to utilize her abilities to avert a possible nuclear disaster, but was Amy the cause in the first place?

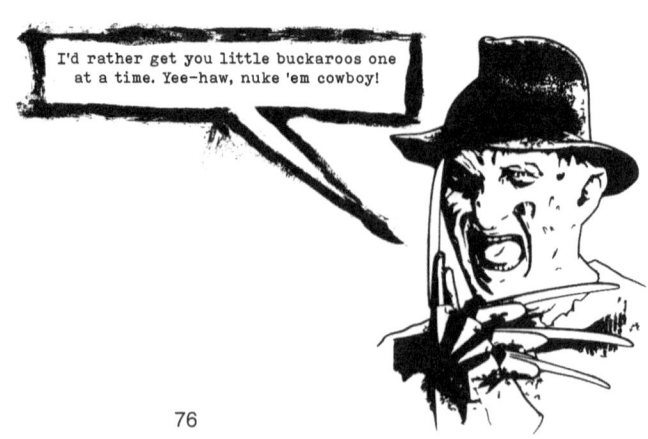

I'd rather get you little buckaroos one at a time. Yee-haw, nuke 'em cowboy!

"Deadline"

Original Air Date: Sunday, January 29, 1989
Season 1, Episode 13

Director: Michael Lange

Writer: Jill Donner

Cast: Page Hannah, Kimiko Gelman, Aaron Harpick, Timothy Brantley, Jenny Gago, Rebecca Stanley, Shelly Kurtz, Dan Gerrity, Jolene Rae, Jeremy Roberts, Brynja McGrady, Robert Englund

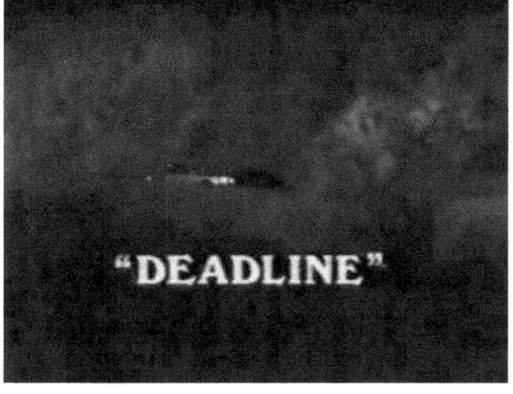

Synopsis

A Story - Peter lands a summer internship at the Springwood Star Times writing obituaries. Peter is disturbed when he starts dreaming of the events surrounding the deaths of those in his columns. Peter tries to quit but his editor won't let a creative mind like his go that easily.

B Story - Guilt-ridden Emily mourns the loss of her friends who were killed in a car accident. Emily is offered the chance to be reunited with them but is horrified when her friends come back from the dead to claim her as well.

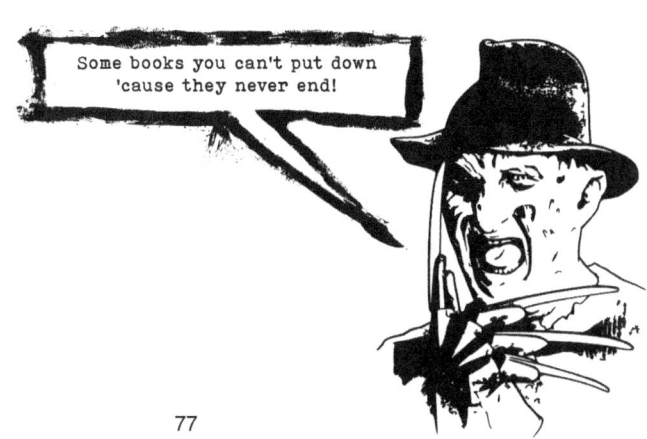

Some books you can't put down 'cause they never end!

"Black Tickets"

Original Air Date: Sunday, February 5, 1989
Season 1, Episode 14

Director: George Kaczender

Writer: Howard Lakin

Cast: Brad Pitt, Kerry Brennan, Karen Hensel, Lora Staley, Kort Falkenberg, Ellen Alberttini, Don Sparks, Bill Moseley, Jeff Austin, Michael Larisey, Jacob Kenner, Robert Englund

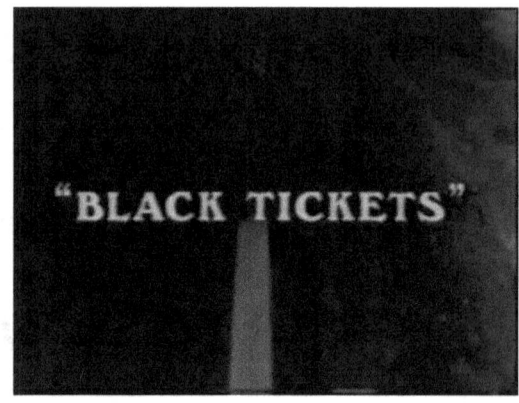

Synopsis

A Story - Rick and Miranda have just eloped and find themselves stranded just outside of Springwood. The two find out that rebellion can have consequences when Springwood refuses to let them leave.

B Story - Miranda lands a job at Springwood Records, but is concerned that she might be pregnant. Unready for the prospect of motherhood, Miranda is confronted by her fears, head on.

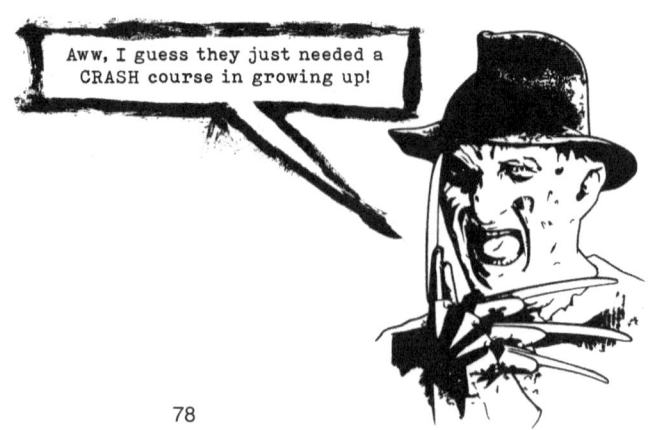

"School Daze"

Original Air Date: Sunday, February 12, 1989
Season 1, Episode 15

Director: Michael Klein

Writer: David Erhman

Cast: Billy Morrissette, Andrew Kraus, James Harper, J. Patrick McNamara, Mitch David Carter, Michael P. Keenan, Lisa Fuller, Nora Masterson, Frank Kopye, David J. Parrington, Warner Loughlin, Robert Englund

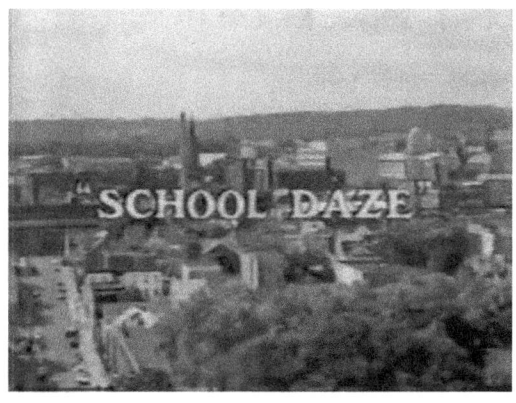

Synopsis

A Story - Steve is an underachiever at Springwood High who is ridiculed by his peers and accused of violating the school's spirit. Steve discovers the dark secret that the school is creating robotic students who obey the rules. Who is man and who is machine?

B Story - Matt is being crushed by the pressure of his impending SAT test. But what is the worst thing that could happen if you bomb the most important test of your life? Matt may be doomed to find out.

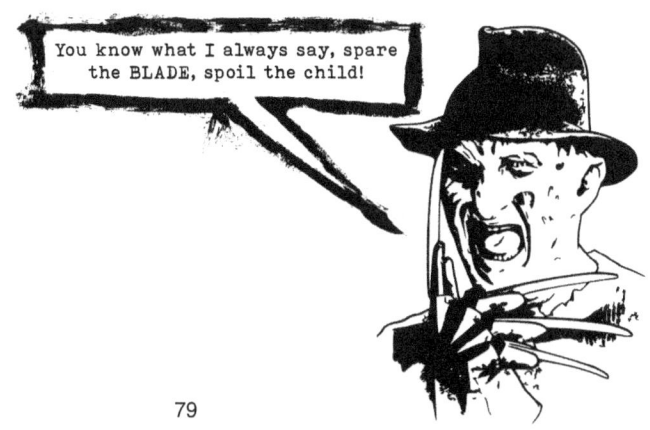

You know what I always say, spare the BLADE, spoil the child!

79

"Cabin Fever"

Original Air Date: Sunday, February 19, 1989
Season 1, Episode 16

Director: Robert Englund

Writer: Rhet Topham

Cast: Brett Cullen, Lezlie Deane, Ted J. Demmers, William Shockley, Bert Hinchman, Robert Englund

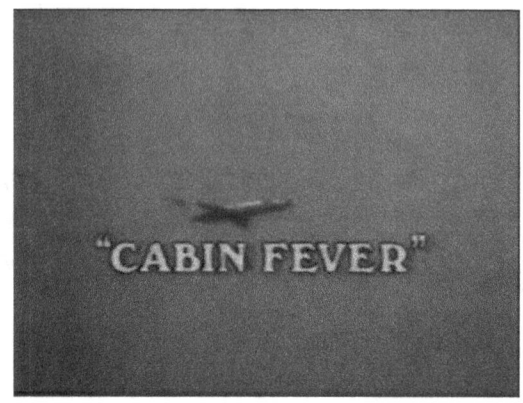

Synopsis

A Story - Carl is afraid of flying and he is about to board a flight of fear to Springwood. Sue tries to keep him calm, but a series of nightmarish visions threaten to drop him right out of the friendly skies.

B Story - Sue is on the lookout for Mr. Right in the local bar when she meets Jim. The two of them decide to head back to Jim's cabin. Jim claims he's not a weirdo, but after all, this is Springwood…

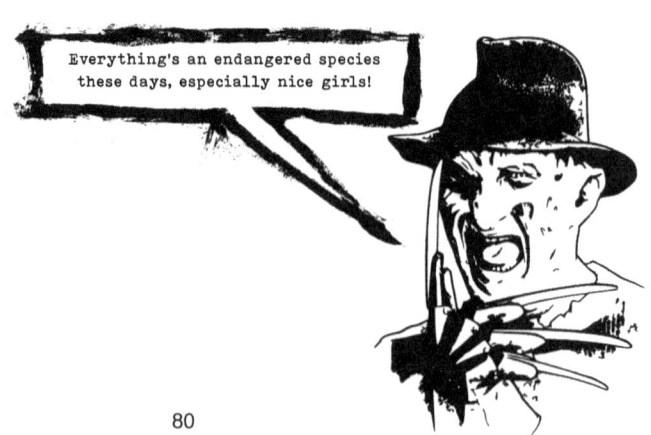

Everything's an endangered species these days, especially nice girls!

"Love Stinks"

Original Air Date: Sunday, February 26, 1989
Season 1, Episode 17

Director: John Lafia

Writers: Michael DeLuca, Jeff Freilich

Cast: Jeffrey Combs, George Olden, John Washington, Susanna Savee, Tamara Glynn, John Medici, Laurie Burton, Stacie Toevs, Bruce Economou, Laura Bastianelli, John Batis, Gil Adler, Robert Englund

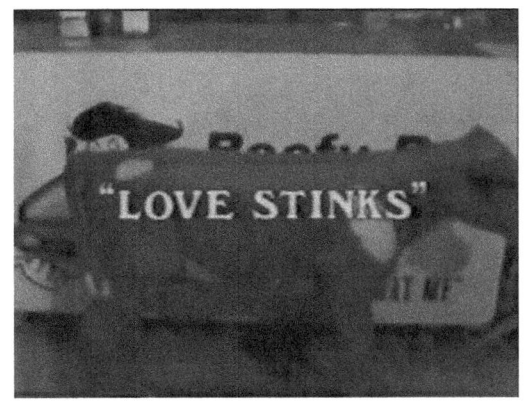

Synopsis

A Story - Adam and his girlfriend Laura are fighting about his unwillingness to declare his love for her. Adam is coerced into a one night stand with Loni, who convinces him to say those three little words that all women want to hear. Little does he know, Loni is looking for something a lot more permanent.

B Story - Max is forced to take a summer job at his uncle's pizza place, Cheesy Boy. Max plans to botch the job and get himself fired, but uncle Ralph has other plans, and a very secret recipe.

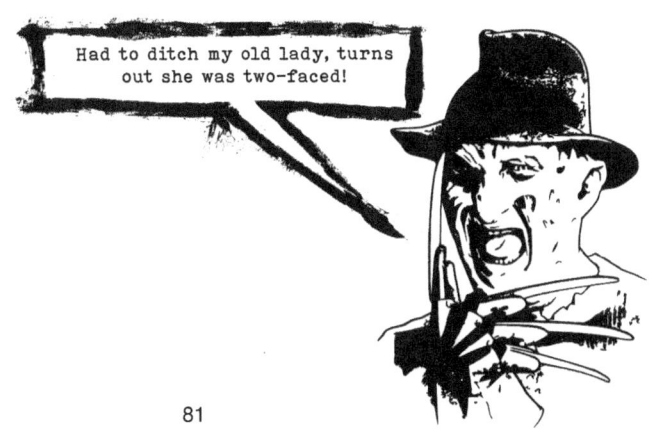

Had to ditch my old lady, turns out she was two-faced!

"The Art of Death"

Original Air Date: Sunday, March 12, 1989
Season 1, Episode 18

Director: Ken Wiederhorn

Writers: Michael DeLuca, Ken Wiederhorn

Cast: Carey Scott, Laura Schaefer, Stuart Fratkin, Leland Holden, Andrew Roperto, Irina Irvine, David Reynolds, Edwina Moore, William Clarke Butler, Michael Watson, Judd Omen, David Renan, Robert Englund

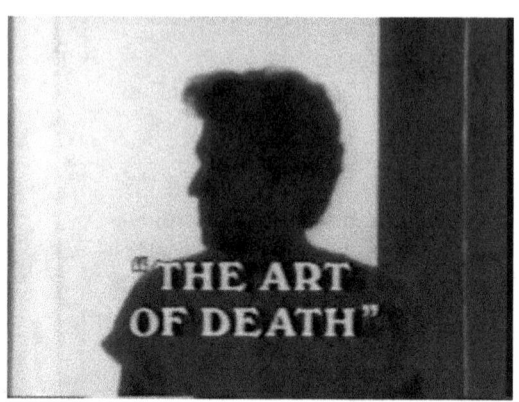

Synopsis

A Story - Jack is an artist with a peculiar talent. When his comic character "The Phantom" comes to life and kidnaps his crush, Joan, Jack must try to regain control over his creation, and his mind.

B Story - Joan is back from her ordeal, but can she keep her sanity when Jamie tries to squeeze out the details of her experience, forcing her to relive the events?

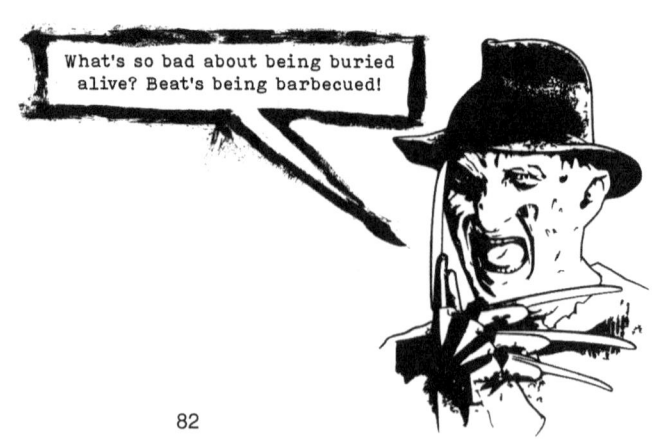

What's so bad about being buried alive? Beat's being barbecued!

"Missing Persons"

Original Air Date: Sunday, May 7, 1989
Season 1, Episode 19

Director: Jeff Freilich

Writer: Jeff Freilich

Cast: Timothy Bottoms, Eva La Rue, Nancy Linari, David Dunard, Sabrina Howells, Bryan Beck, Elliot Easton, Erica Horne, Rodney Saulsberry, Hans Howes, Robert Englund

Synopsis

A Story - Formerly obese Gina returns to her childhood home to babysit the Franklin's two children, Dolly and Ricky. After the Franklin's leave for the evening, things start to go off-center as the children's obsession with junk food begins to eat away at Gina's sanity.

B Story - Ken is having a mid-life crisis and wishes that he could be someone else. Abducted at gunpoint, Ken is thrust into a high speed criminal lifestyle running from the cops, before finally crashing back into reality.

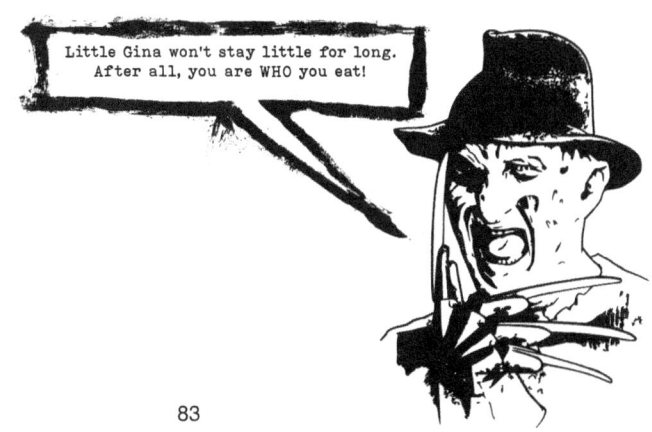

Little Gina won't stay little for long. After all, you are WHO you eat!

"The Light at the End of the Tunnel"

Original Air Date: Sunday, May 14, 1989
Season 1, Episode 20

Director: Jonathan Betuel

Writers: James Cappe, Jonathan Betuel

Cast: Steven Keats, David Arnott, Dick Miller, Dana Stevens, Stephen Burks, Lisa Raphael, Jamie McEnnan, Greg Davis, Vraig Berenson, Heather Jane MacDonald, Pamela Kayt, Luce Morgan, Kenyatta Poul, Marty Pollio, Robert Englund

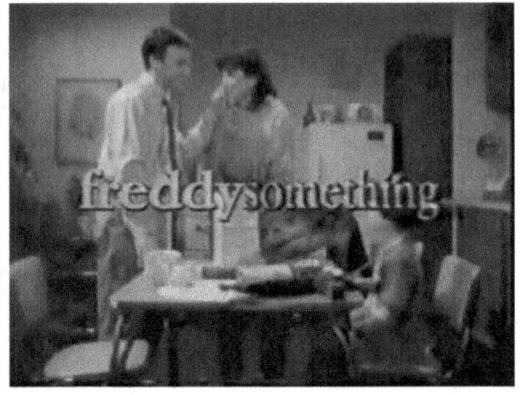

Synopsis

A Story - Michael is unemployed and striking out on job interviews. He finally finds success and lands a job working in the sewers of Springwood. There's just one problem, Michael is afraid of the dark and something monstrous is lurking in the tunnels below.

B Story - Murray is the stubborn manager of Springwood Video. One night a mysterious businessman gives him a prototype subliminal messaging self help videotape. Murray soon finds out that the tape's message is much more sinister.

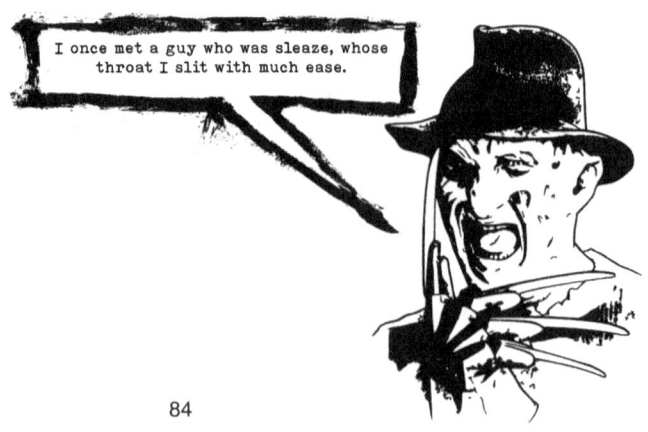

I once met a guy who was sleaze, whose throat I slit with much ease.

"Identity Crisis"

Original Air Date: Sunday, May 21, 1989
Season 1, Episode 21

Director: David Calloway

Writer: Rebecca Pogrow

Cast: Jeff Conaway, Gabe Jarret, Kimberley Kates, Patricia Estrin, Hank Stratton, Patricia Lee Wilson, David Kagen, Jacqueline Daniels, Walter Caldwell, Robert Englund

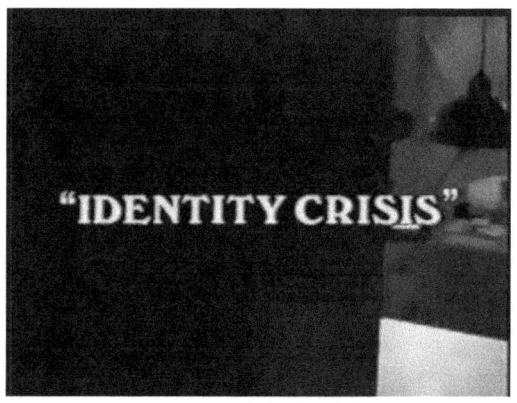

Synopsis

A Story - Buddy is turning forty and everyone around him begins to treat him like an old obsolete piece of machinery. Buddy wants a do-over on life, but in Springwood it's "out with the old, in with the new."

B Story - Christina feels like she doesn't belong in her family and has recurring dreams about being adopted from a deranged orphanage as a child. Christina starts to suspect that her dreams are actually memories and confronts her mother about who her real parents were, but the truth may be a nightmare of its own.

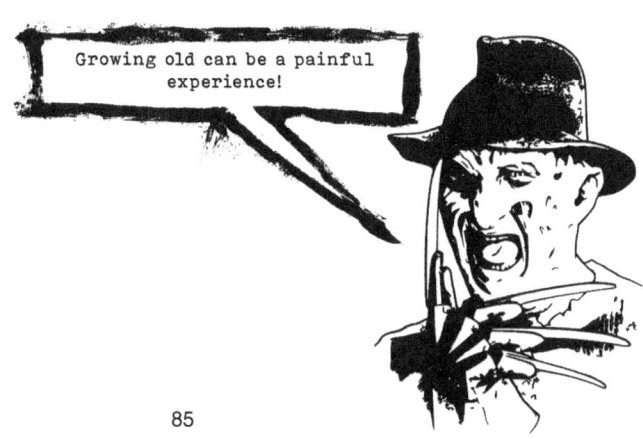

Growing old can be a painful experience!

"Safe Sex"

Original Air Date: Sunday, May 28, 1989
Season 1, Episode 22

Director: Jerry Olsen

Writer: David J. Schow

Cast: Devon Pierce, Patrick Day, Andy Woodworth, Jake Jacobs, Arlene Banas, Kristine Blackburn, Sanford Clark, Darrell Kunitomi, Ron Troncatty, Robert Englund

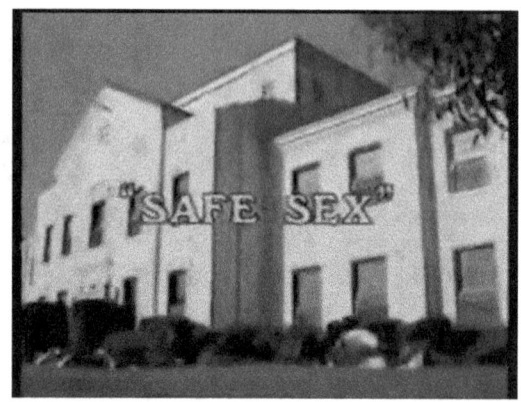

Synopsis

A Story - Dana is a high school virgin who lusts after foxy goth girl Caitlin, who happens to have an obsession of her own. Caitlin turns out to be much more than Dana can handle and losing his virginity isn't everything he had dreamed of.

B Story - Caitlin thinks she has found the man of her dreams, but when Freddy puts the moves on her, her dreams become nightmares as she realizes that they aren't as alike as she had previously thought.

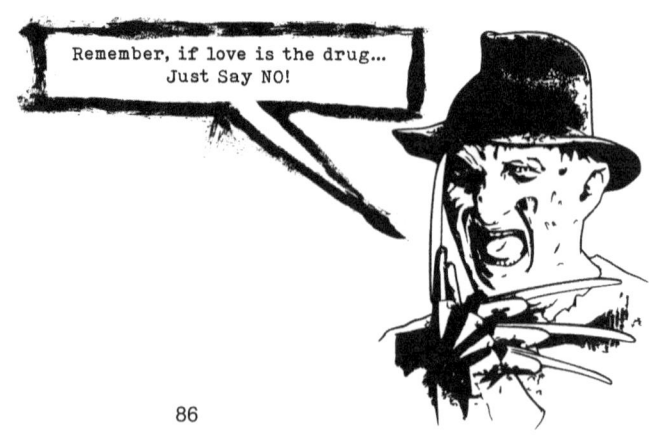

Remember, if love is the drug...
Just Say NO!

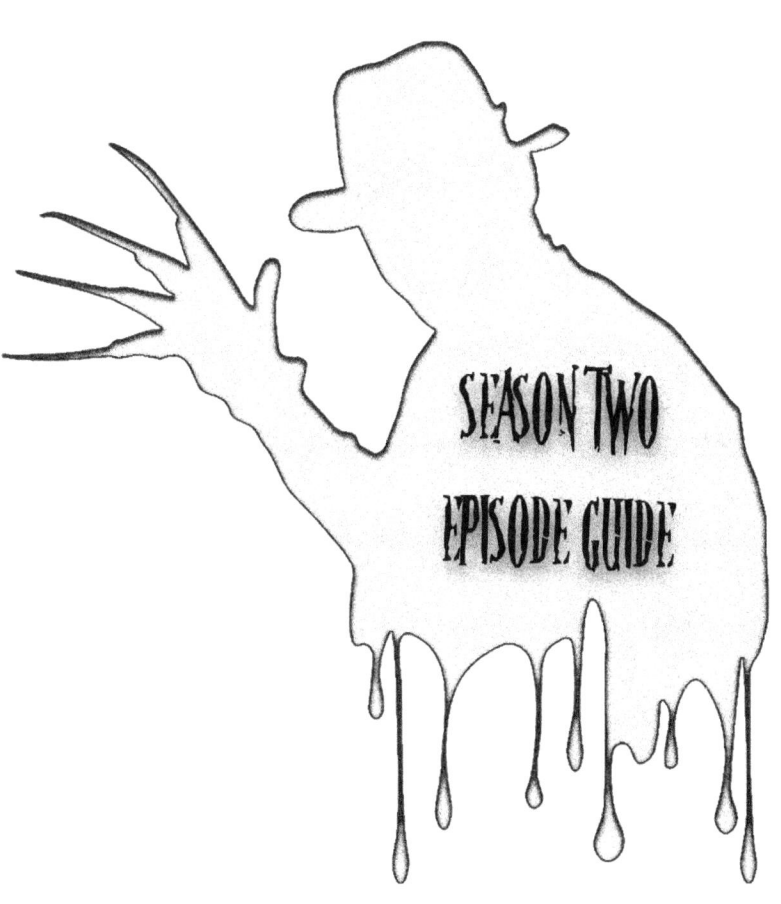

SEASON TWO

EPISODE GUIDE

"Dream Come True"

Original Air Date: Sunday, October 8, 1989
Season 2, Episode 1

Director: George Kaczender

Writers: Tom Blomquist, Tom Lazarus

Cast: David Kaufman, Scott Marlowe, Linda Miller, Gerard Prendergast, R. Leo Schreiber, Charles Cyphers, Bruce Marchiano, Jay Thomas, George Sims, Robert Englund

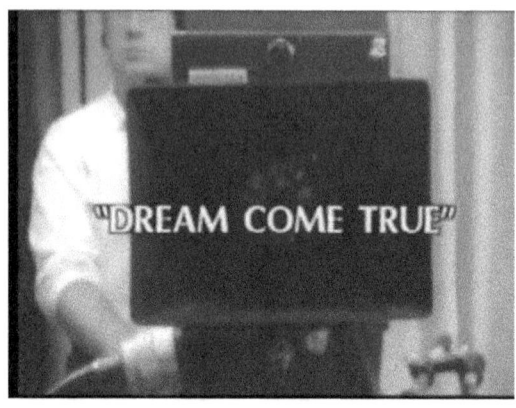

Synopsis

A Story - Randy is the perfect candidate for Dr. Kefler's "Dream Come True" therapy given his refusal to sleep due to ongoing nightmares. Dr. Kefler attempts to exorcise Randy's dream demon, but you can't keep a good nightmare phantom down as Freddy turns his sights on the Doc himself.

B Story - Television journalist, Gary, thinks he has the biggest story of his career when he cracked the case of all the mysterious murders in Springwood. Attempting to prove that Freddy is still alive and killing may just seal Gary's own fate.

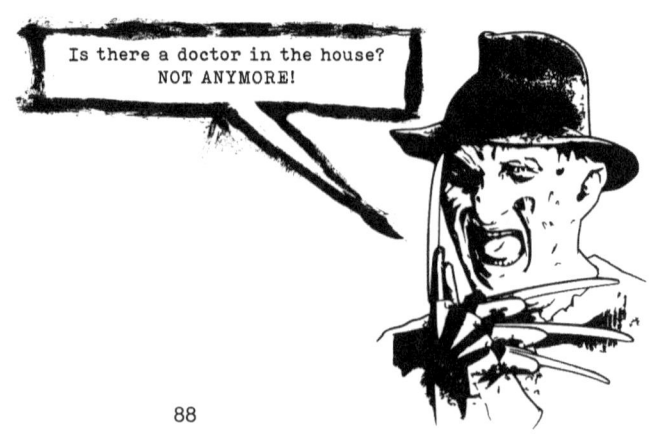

Is there a doctor in the house?
NOT ANYMORE!

"Heartbreak Hotel"

Original Air Date: Sunday, October 15, 1989
Season 2, Episode 2

Director: William Malone

Writer: Jonathan Glassner

Cast: Terri Semper, Gloria Loring, John Stinson, Tiffany Helm, Owen Bush, Stacey Keach Sr., Jack Mannings, Patty Toy, Katsy Chappell, Anne Lockhart, Richard Cox, Jay Boryea, Robert Englund

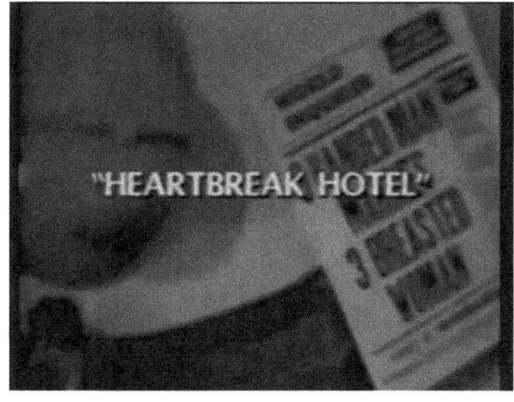

Synopsis

A Story - Roger is a reporter for the tabloid newspaper World Enquirer and is about to land a serious career boost working for a legitimate paper. For his last assignment at the Enquirer, Roger is sent to Springwood to investigate a mysterious sighting… of Elvis Presley. Once in Springwood, Roger finds that Elvis may not be in Springwood, but there is definitely something strange afoot as his writing starts to come true.

B Story - Jerry is in a car accident and winds up in the hospital with amnesia. As his memories start to return, Jerry becomes concerned that he may have committed murder before the accident.

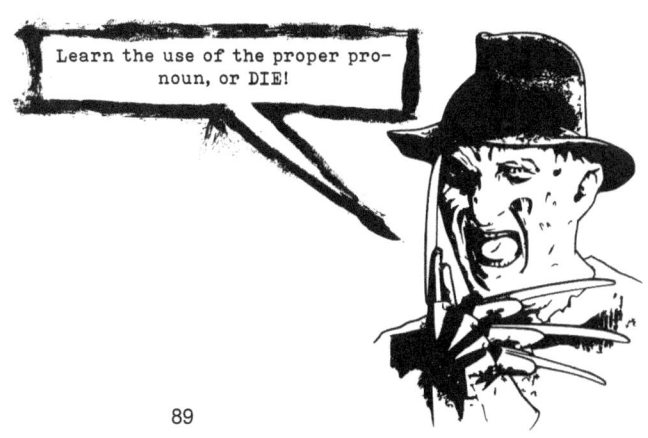

Learn the use of the proper pronoun, or DIE!

"Welcome to Springwood"

Original Air Date: Sunday, October 22, 1989
Season 2, Episode 3

Director: Ken Wiederhorn

Writers: Alan Katz, Gil Adler

Cast: Leah Ayres, Michael Horton, George Kmeck, Todd Allen, Dey Young, Camilla Ashlend, Webster Williams, Brenda Cooper, Robert Englund

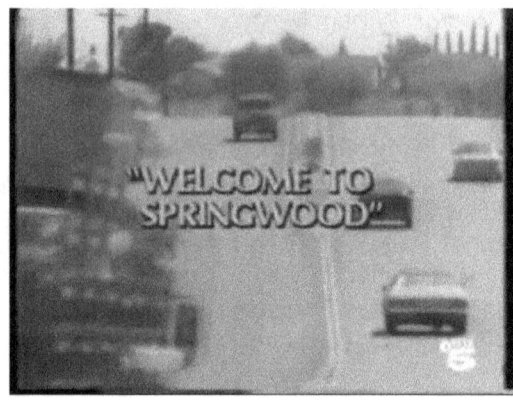

Synopsis

A Story - Doug and Roxanne relocate to Springwood. When Roxanne begins unpacking she finds a gruesome collection of bloody clothes and knives. Convinced that there has been a mix-up with the moving company, Roxanne begins to have nightmares about the owner of the items. As the truth unfolds, she learns the horrifying truth about the true owner of the items.

B Story - Emily has just moved into a new apartment when she discovers a collection of 19th century love letters. As she continues to read the letters she becomes entwined in a ghostly love triangle with a vengeful apparition.

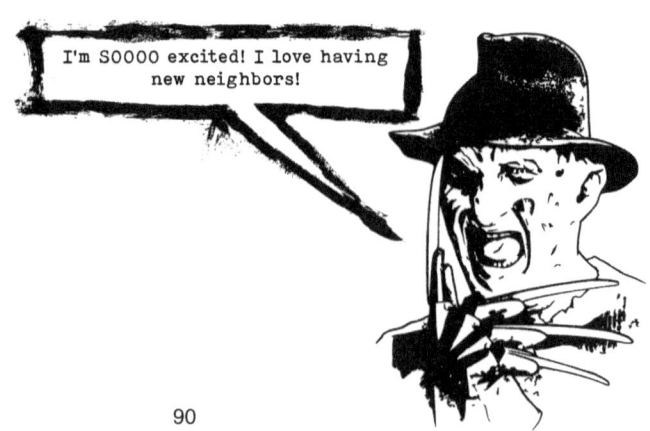

"Photo Finish"

Original Air Date: Sunday, October 29, 1989
Season 2, Episode 4

Director: Tom DeSimone

Writer: Bill Froelich

Cast: Patty McCormack, Lareine Chabut, Lisa Aliff, Gay Thomas, Kristina Loggia, Richard Speight, Patrick Waddell, Vivien Strauss, Shauna McCoy, D. David Morin, Jason Wingreen, Warren Burton, Robert Englund

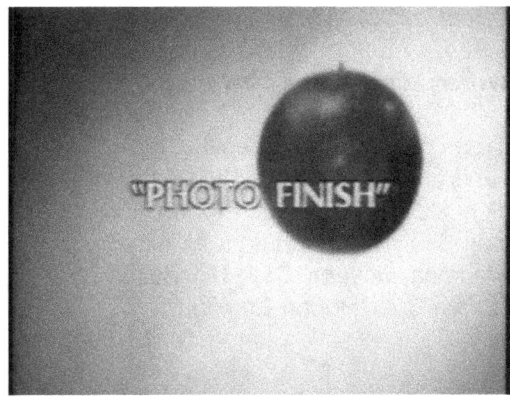

Synopsis

A Story - Stoney Adler is a down on her luck fashion photographer who taking family portraits to make ends meet. When she's offered a career boosting gig for the Halloween issue of KINK she jumps at the opportunity. Unfortunately for her, Freddy shows up to take over the shoot.

B Story - It's Halloween in Springwood and the FBI has been called in to investigate a brutal family murder. When the agents recreates the crime a little too realistically, Freddy shows up to tamper with the evidence.

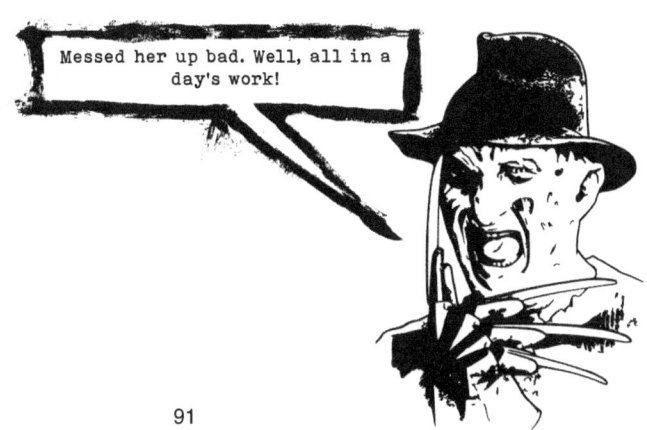

"Memory Overload"

Original Air Date: Sunday, November 5, 1989
Season 2, Episode 5

Director: Don Weis

Writer: Michael Kirschenbaum

Cast: Sharon Mahoney, Daren Landry, Andrew Prine, Kyle Chandler, Alex Cord, Dean Denton, Eileen Seely, Vincent Leahr, Winifred Freeman, Joseph Cali, Bill Baker, Lauren Cole, Robert Englund

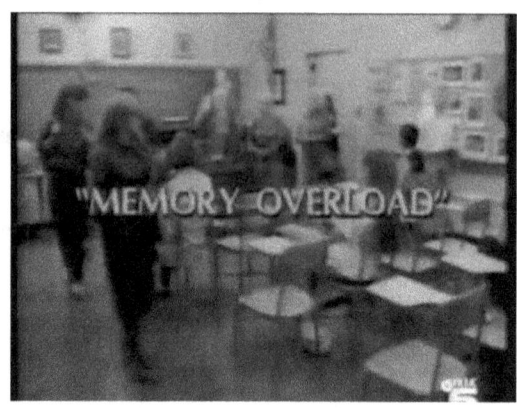

Synopsis

A Story - Charles Winton is an alcoholic college professor. When his former student, Chuck, deserts the army, he comes to the professor for help. While Winton is hiding Chuck he starts to improve himself, becoming clean and sober, and simultaneously Chuck's mental state withers, but when Chuck's father shows up the professor's front begins to unravel.

B Story - Barbara is a vindictive credit rater at Comput-A-Credit with zero tolerance for customer service. But when she chooses to help those close to her instead of people with real problems her computer comes to life to level the playing field and teach Barbara a lesson in humility.

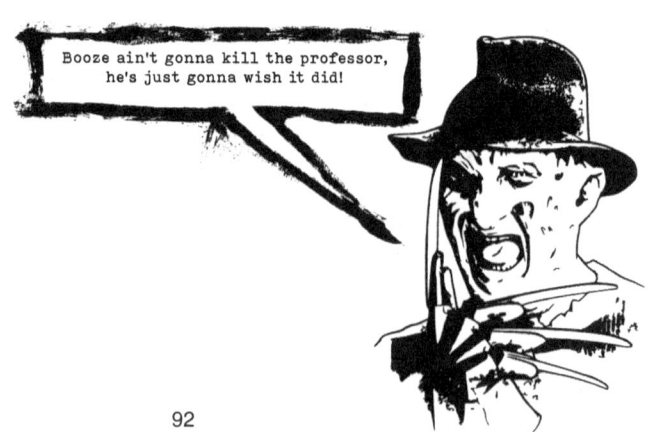

Booze ain't gonna kill the professor, he's just gonna wish it did!

92

"Lucky Stiff"

Original Air Date: Sunday, November 12, 1989
Season 2, Episode 6

Director: William Malone

Writer: David Braff

Cast: David Lander, Mary Crosby, Richard Eden, Perri Lister, Frank Birney, Tracy Walter, Glen Vernon, Robert Englund

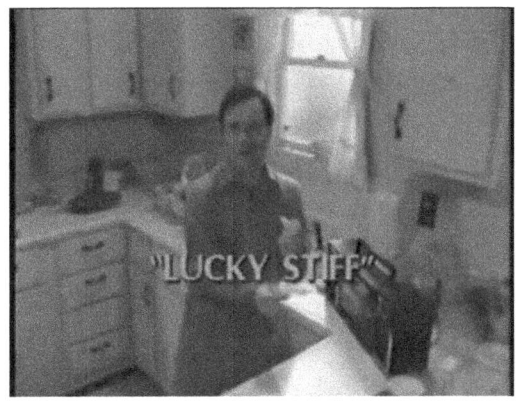

Synopsis

A Story - Greta is having an affair with Hank and she is planning to leave her husband, Lenny, but he dies from a heart attack before she gets the chance. Greta then marries Hank and after hearing a news story about an unclaimed lottery she realizes that the winning ticket is in the pocket of the suit that they buried Lenny in.

B Story - Greta has moved up in the world and is enjoying the good life when she's informed that someone had called claiming to be her husband. A concerned Greta returns to Springwood Cemetery to find that Hank's body was not in the tomb where she had left him.

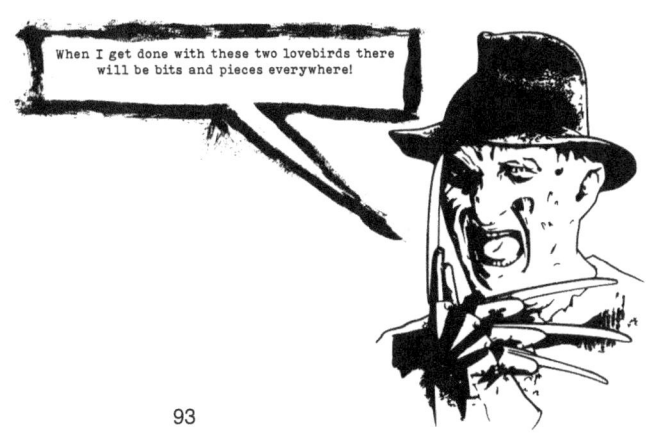

"Silence is Golden"

Original Air Date: Sunday, November 19, 1989
Season 2, Episode 7

Director: Chuck Braverman

Writer: Jonathan Glassner

Cast: Jeff Yagher, Sherry Hursey, Gretchen Palmer, Steve Franken, Phil Esposito, Joseph di Reda, Craig Peters, Albie Selznick, Kim Morgan Greene, Bart Braverman, Kendall Carly Browne, Robert Englund

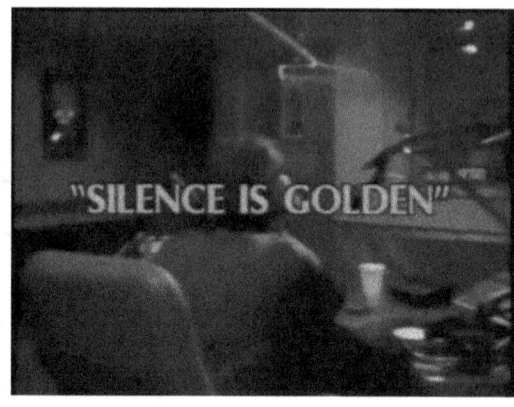

Synopsis

A Story - Shock jock DJ Rick Rake is a loud mouth with a hot temper. When he mistakenly punches a mime on the street, he learns a valuable lesson about keeping your mouth shut.

B Story - Kip is a mime by day and a jewel thief by night. His latest robbery goes off without a hitch, that is until he learns that the homeowners have been murdered and he is being framed for the crime.

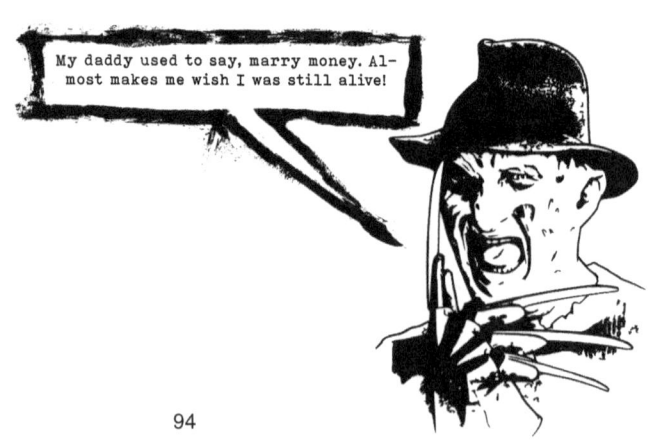

My daddy used to say, marry money. Almost makes me wish I was still alive!

"Bloodlines"

Original Air Date: Sunday, November 26, 1989
Season 2, Episode 8

Director: James Quinn

Writers: Alan Katz, Gil Adler

Cast: Sheree North, Chris Nash, Marc Alaimo, Ruth DeSosa, Melanie Tomlin, Irina Chasen, Walter Addison, Ed Lottimer, Robert Englund

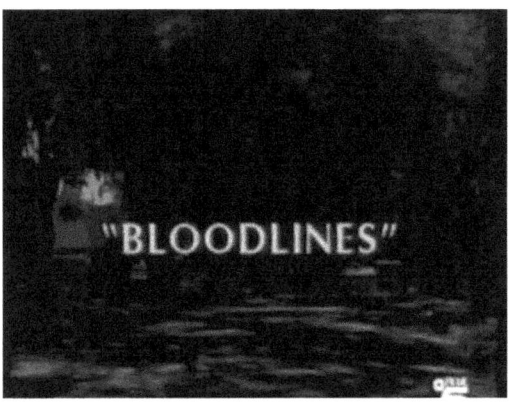

Synopsis

A Story - Woody has just broken out of prison and returns home to retrieve his cache of stolen money only to find that his son, Jack, had found and moved the cash. Woody hits Jack with his pistol and thinking that he killed him takes his body out to bury it with his other victim. But what Woody doesn't realize is that the grave he's digging just might be his own.

B Story - Jack and Maggie want a baby but Maggie is unable to conceive. Jack uses his father's stolen money to purchase a baby for the couple. Maggie starts to wonder just what kind of a family would put their child up for sale and what sinister effect that would have on little baby Patty as her behavior spirals out of control.

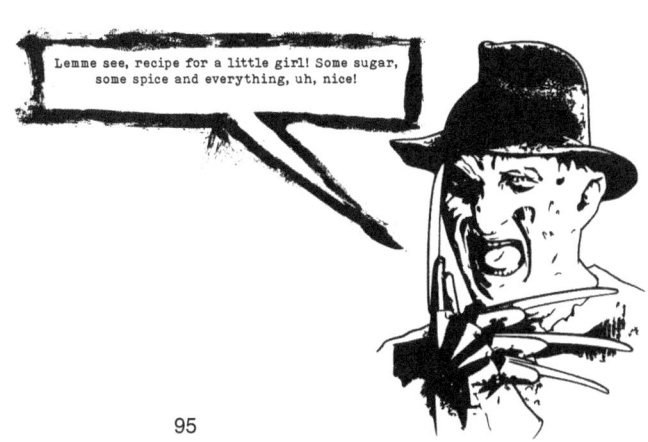

Lemme see, recipe for a little girl! Some sugar, some spice and everything, uh, nice!

"Monkey Dreams"

Original Air Date: Sunday, December 3, 1989
Season 2, Episode 9

Director: Robert Englund

Writer: Michael Kirschenbaum

Cast: Joe Cali, Rick Dano, Sharon Mahoney, Sherman Howard, Eileen Seely, Rick Zumwalt, Charles Champion, Alan Berger, Robert Englund

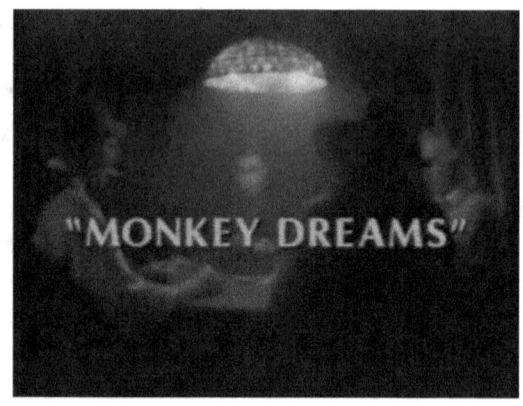

Synopsis

A Story - Joe is a gambler who's racked up quite the debt. Joe hatches a scheme to get rich quick, but things don't go according to plan and it's time for Joe to settle up.

B Story - Dr. Lynch is performing cruel experiments on chimpanzee Winston and is being harassed by animal rights activists. Dr. Lynch has a change of heart only to backpedal later as he becomes the subject of Winston's nightmares.

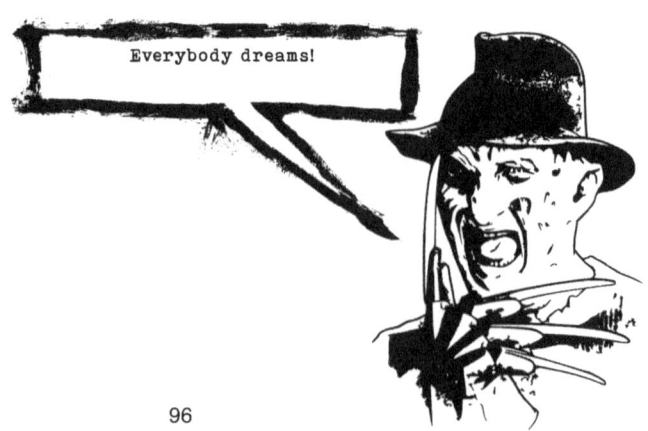

Everybody dreams!

"Do You Know Where Your Kids Are?"

Original Air Date: Sunday, December 10, 1989
Season 2, Episode 10

Director: Bill Froelich

Writer: Wayne Allan Rice

Cast: Courtney Gebhart, Suzanne Tara, Sharron Farrell, Julie St. Claire, Jeannie Lewis, Chris Nash, Chris Finefrock, Brad Hunt, Robert Englund

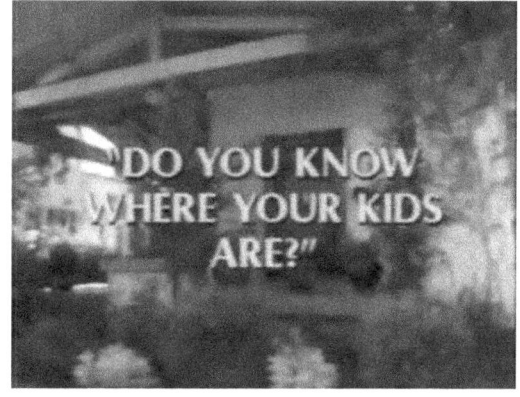

Synopsis

A Story - Lisa agrees to fill in for Heidi babysitting for the Burtons. Upon arriving Lisa is told that everything will be fine as long as she doesn't open the basement door. Lisa soon learns that the Burtons have locked their monstrous daughter, Patty, in the basement. In a bizarre turn of events of events, Lisa and Patty end up switching places.

B Story - One month later, Lisa's mother shows up at the Burton's house revealing that Lisa has been missing since a car accident on the night that she had babysat for them, all the while not knowing that Lisa has been trapped in the Burton's basement the whole time.

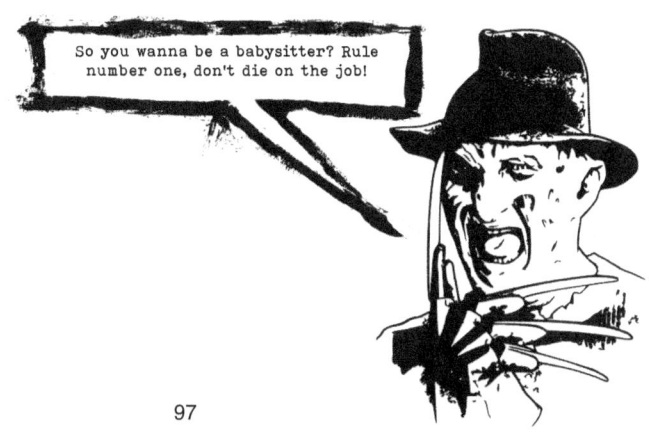

So you wanna be a babysitter? Rule number one, don't die on the job!

"Dreams that Kill"

Original Air Date: Sunday, December 17, 1989
Season 2, Episode 11

Director: Tom DeSimone

Writer: Tom Blomquist

Cast: Dick Gautier, Brian Sheehan, Deborah Rennard, Christina Belford, Nicholas Cascone, Christian Bocher, Bobby Furguson, Don Perry, Phyllis Franklin, Nicholas Gunn, Delores Mitchell, Alan Altshuld, Marsha Burrs, Robert Englund

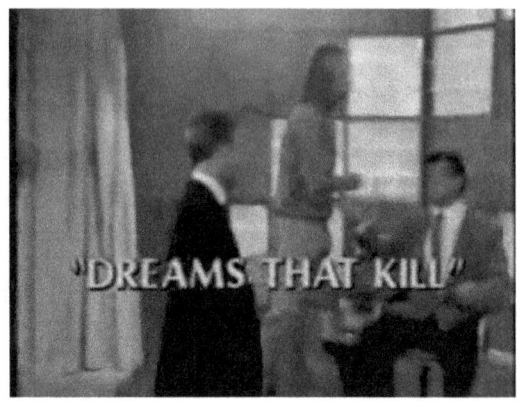

Synopsis

A Story - Charlie is the new host of the TV show "Springwood Confidential," after announcing his upcoming episode "Dreams that Kill" investigating the dream related deaths in Springwood, Charlie comes face to face with the man behind the killings, Freddy Krueger.

B Story - Charlie is in the hospital in a coma and when a young motorcycle accident victim, Mike, is brought into the emergency room, Dr. Erwin secretly transplants tissue from Charlie's healthy brain into the nearly brain dead Mike as part of an experimental procedure. Mike makes a miraculous recovery, but in addition to regaining his brain function he has also inherited an unwanted nightmare parasite.

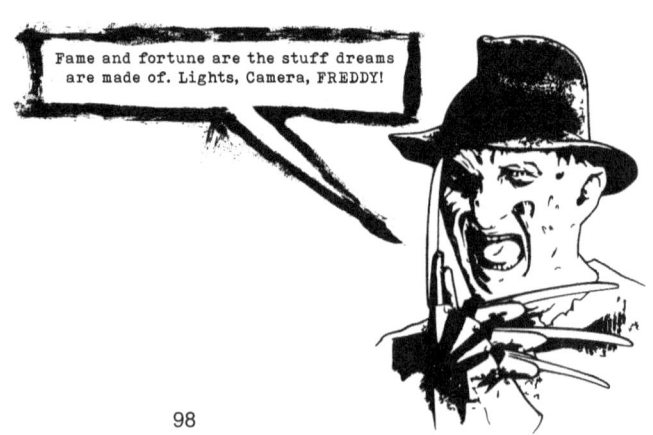

Fame and fortune are the stuff dreams are made of. Lights, Camera, FREDDY!

"It's My Party and You'll Die if I Want You To"

Original Air Date: Sunday, December 24, 1989
Season 2, Episode 12

Director: Tom DeSimone

Writer: David Braff

Cast: Francois Giroday, Greg Monaghan, Barbara Treutelaar, Joy Baggish, Gwen Banta, LeReine Chabut, John Fujioka, Russel Lunday, Nicholas Shaffer, Richard Speight Jr., Vivien Straus, Patrick Waddell, Robert Englund

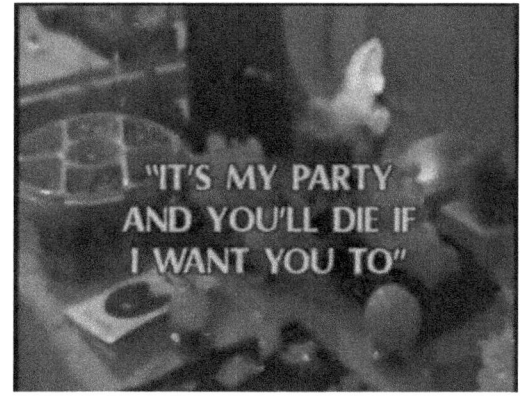

Synopsis

A Story - Mara is a bogus psychic pretending to channel the dead at the Springwood New Age Convention. She goes into a trance and becomes possessed by Freddy. As he controls her body in the real world, Mara's mind is stuck in the boiler room of Freddy's dream domain.

B Story - The Springwood Hotel is hosting Springwood High's Class of 1970 twenty year reunion. With only nineteen classmates left alive, Freddy crashes the party to take care of the rest.

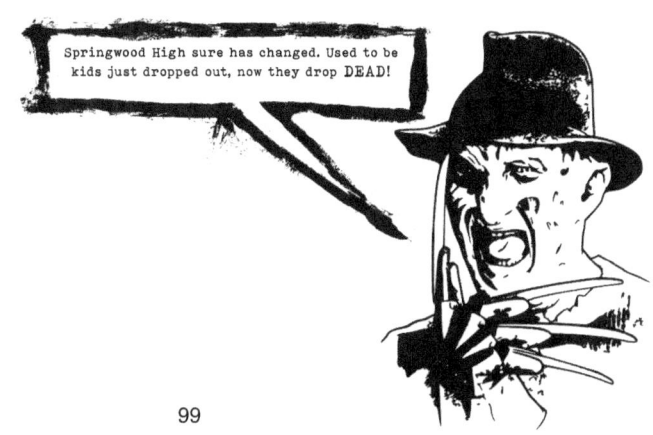

Springwood High sure has changed. Used to be kids just dropped out, now they drop DEAD!

"What You Don't Know Can Kill You"

Original Air Date: Sunday, January 7, 1990
Season 2, Episode 13

Director: Ken Wiederhorn

Writer: Jonathan Glassner

Cast: Philip Proctor, Rosalind In-gledew, David Hern, Fran Monta-no, Rochelle Carson, Paul Regina, Mary Gillis, Jovin Montanaro, Ken Zavayna, Roger Kern, Michael Gregory, Robert Englund

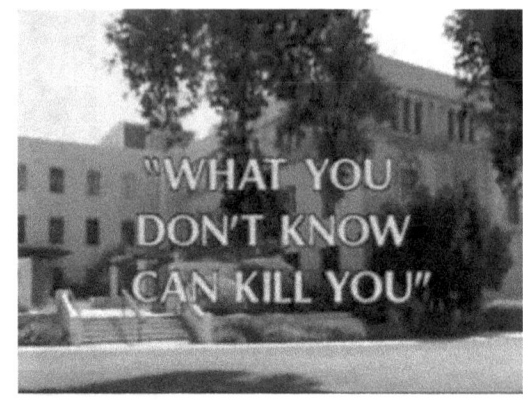

Synopsis

A Story - Dr. Donald Crowley is a sleazy hypnotherapist who takes advantage of his female patients. When he is caught in the act by colleague, Dr. Rothman, Crowley hypnotizes a new patient, Derby, and uses him to take care of the evidence.

B Story - Derby begins to realize what he had done under hypnosis and his girl-friend Helen convinces him to get plastic surgery to hide from the authorities. But when he adorns the face of a mobster turned state's evidence he finds himself on the run from a mob hitman.

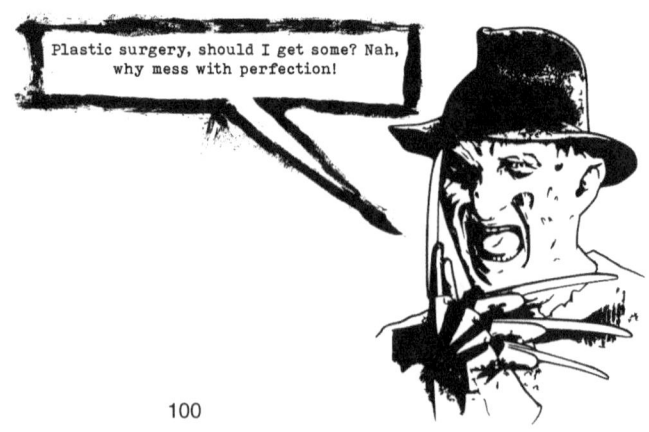

Plastic surgery, should I get some? Nah, why mess with perfection!

"Easy Come, Easy Go"

Original Air Date: Sunday, January 14, 1990
Season 2, Episode 14

Director: William Malone

Writers: David Braff

Cast: Mary Crosby, Tracey Walter, Wings Hauser, Richard Eden, Jill Jacobson, Frank Birney, Robert Englund

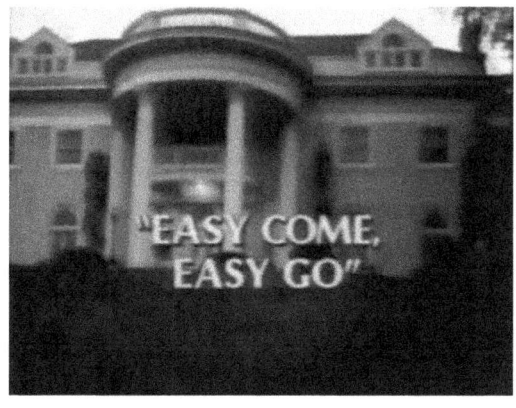

Synopsis

A Story - Greta has the body of her ex-husband Hank in her freezer. When Hank's brother, Wes, shows up, he and Greta cook up a scheme to off her new husband Eugene, but after finding Hank in the freezer, Wes turns his sights on Greta. Eugene saves the day, but the celebration is short lived.

B Story - Greta has three bodies in her basement and is about to skip town with twenty million dollars when her sister and her new husband show up for a surprise visit. Greta soon finds out that her sister also has some skeletons in the closet.

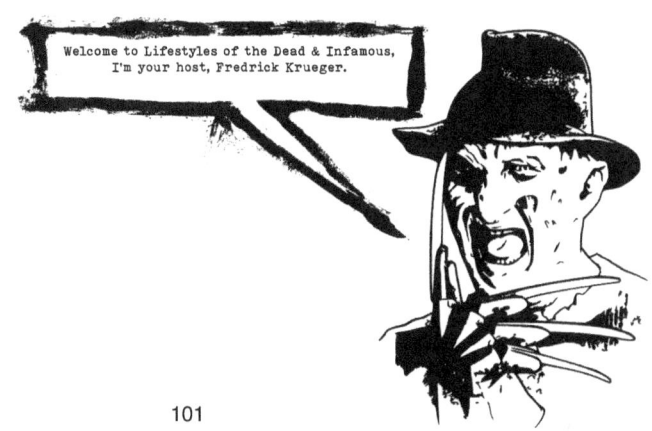

Welcome to Lifestyles of the Dead & Infamous, I'm your host, Fredrick Krueger.

"Prime Cut"

Original Air Date: Sunday, January 21, 1990
Season 2, Episode 15

Director: David Calloway

Writers: Michael Kirschenbaum

Cast: Tony Dow, Sandahl Berg-man, Chris Stanley, Amy Lyndon, Donovan Scott, Herman Poppe, Doug Dupuy, Charles Young, Rob-ert Englund

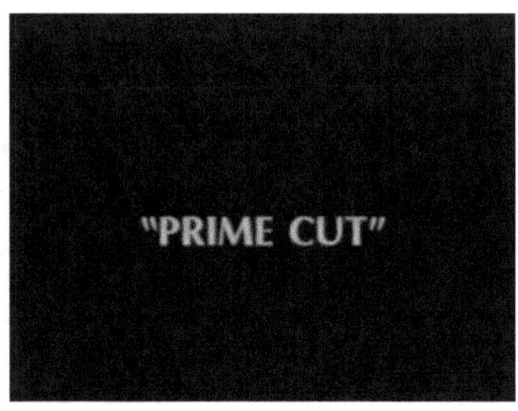

Synopsis

A Story - Johnny, Jake and Todd are in Springwood Forest on a hunting excursion led by Ginger "Tracker" Morgan. When Tracker begins to act strangely Johnny starts to suspect that she might be a vampire, but the twisted wreckage of the truth may be much worse.

B Story - Johnny and Tracker are stuck in a ravine with their downed aircraft and are forced to eat the flesh of their dead friends. When the search is called off Johnny's fiancée Mary Beth heads out on her own, but what she finds may be too much to stomach.

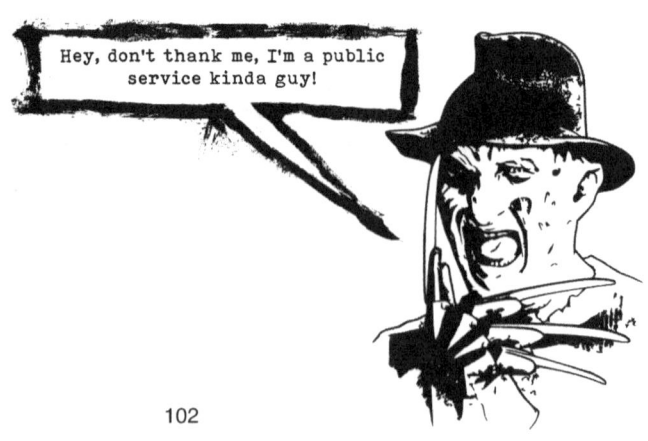

Hey, don't thank me, I'm a public service kinda guy!

"Interior Loft"

Original Air Date: Sunday, January 28, 1990
Season 2, Episode 16

Director: Ken Wiederhorn

Writers: David Braff

Cast: Robert F. Lyons, Fabiana Udenio, Margot Rose, Dean Fortunato, Kenneth David Gilman, Elizabeth Keifer, Craig Richard Nelson, Eric Stromer, Clifton Gonzales Collins, Sandra Sexton, John DiSanti, Robert Englund

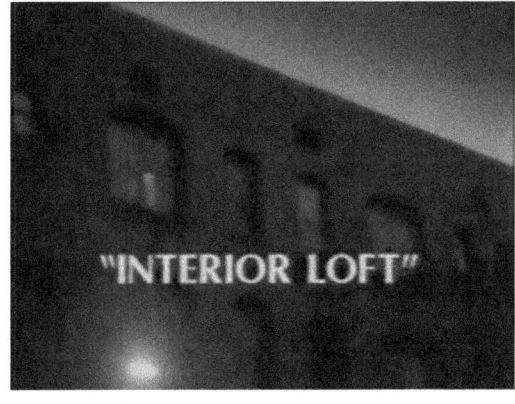

Synopsis

A Story - David convinces his girlfriend Kim to do a 976 phone line for extra money and when their recording appears to inspire a killer Kim must navigate the police and an obsessive stalker.

B Story - Kim is writing a novel called "Killer Sex," when David reads her manuscript he starts to think that Kim is living out the fantasy world in real life and that he might be in actual danger.

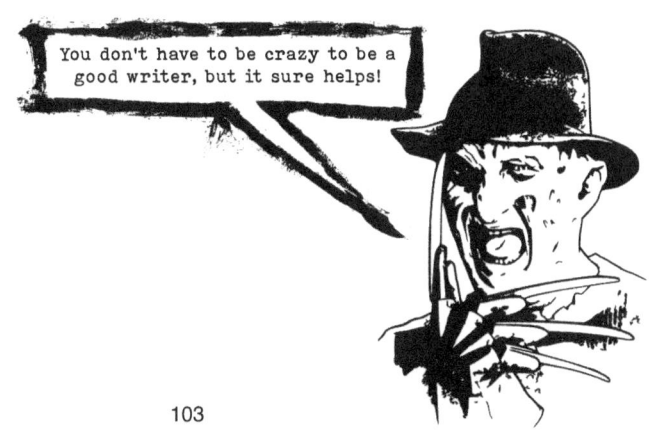

You don't have to be crazy to be a good writer, but it sure helps!

"Interior Loft Later"

Original Air Date: Sunday, February 4, 1990
Season 2, Episode 17

Director: Ken Wiederhorn

Writers: Jonathan Glassner

Cast: Kenneth David Gilman, Elizabeth Keifer, Ron Max, Dean Fortunato, Leslie Bega, Tory Polone, Michael Tierney, Brad Burlingame, Tracy Pulliam, Michael Black, Robert Englund

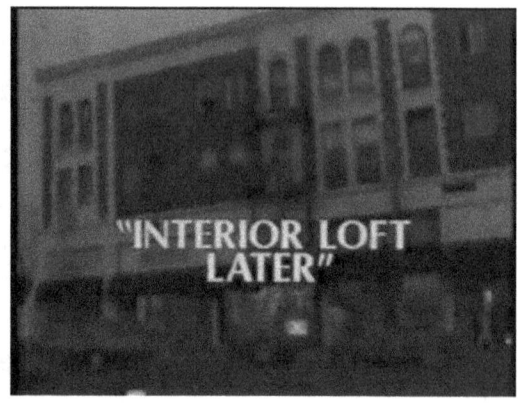

Synopsis

A Story - In Springwood, art imitates death when Alex, a struggling artist, decides to fake his own death in order to increase the value of his work. While Alex is hiding out, he starts to lose his grip on reality.

B Story - Gina and Stacey take a gamble and let Art move into their apartment with them. But when his stories don't seem to add up the ladies wonder if Art may be more dangerous than he seemed.

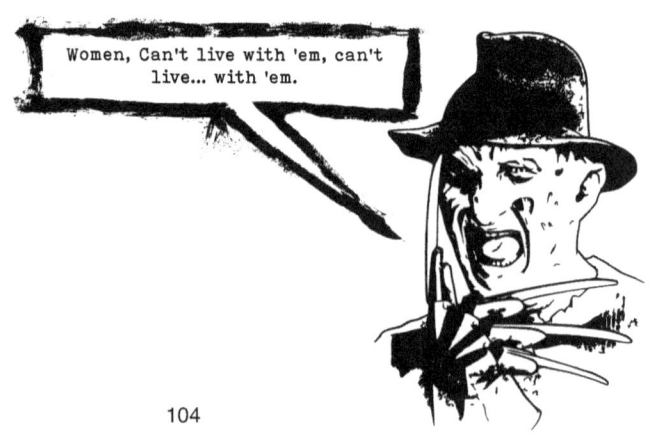

Women, Can't live with 'em, can't live... with 'em.

"Funhouse"

Original Air Date: Sunday, February 11, 1990
Season 2, Episode 18

Director: Gil Adler

Writers: Alan Katz, Gil Adler

Cast: Clayton Landey, Todd Allen, Robin Greer, Joseph Brutsman, Valerie Wildman, Laura Austin, Robert Dowdell, Robert Englund

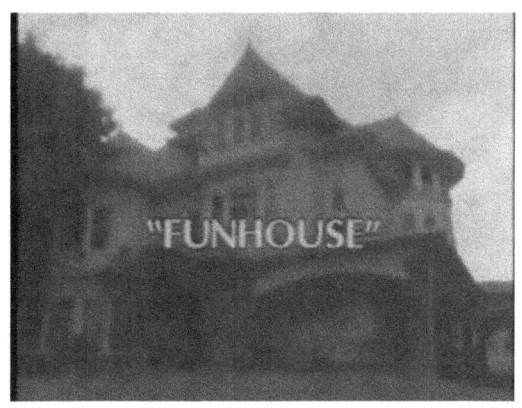

Synopsis

A Story - Emma and Robert have just moved into an old Victorian mansion in Springwood and soon discover that their new home is haunted when a vengeful spirit attempts to seduce Emma.

B Story - Evelyn and her invalid husband Victor have moved into the mansion, but when Evelyn becomes involved with Turk, the moving man, Turk learns that things aren't always what they seem.

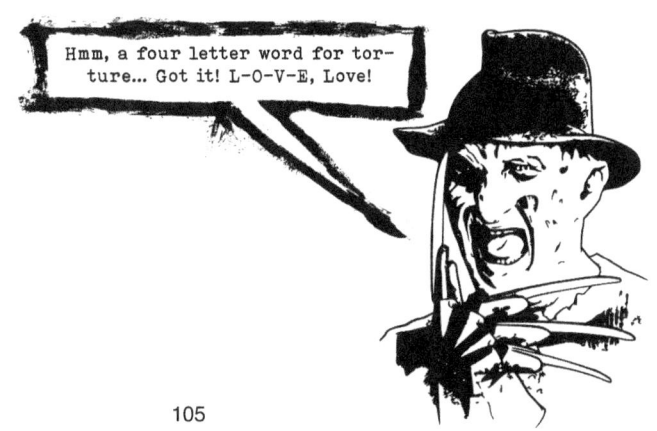

Hmm, a four letter word for torture... Got it! L-O-V-E, Love!

"A Family Affair"

Original Air Date: Sunday, February 18, 1990
Season 2, Episode 19

Director: Keith Samples

Writers: David Braff

Cast: Leonard O. Turner, Kim Morgan Greene, Marlene Warfield, Morris Chestnut, Leonard Donato, Gina Gallego, Robert Englund

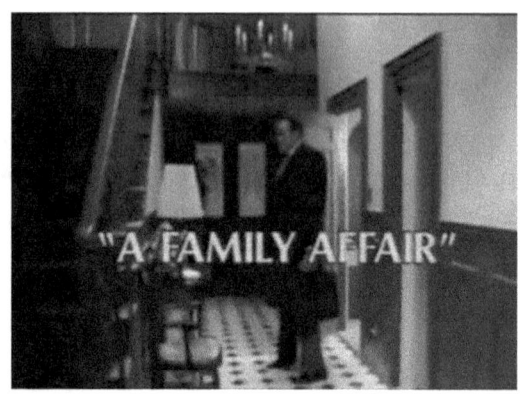

Synopsis

A Story - Paul Woodman is cheating on his wife, but when he doesn't want to fully commit to his mistress she goes off the deep end. Paul hatches a plan to take care of her, but Claire has plans of her own.

B Story - Two years later, Paul suffers a heart attack and must attempt to reconcile with his estranged son Jason. But when Claire returns, the stakes get higher and the game, deadly.

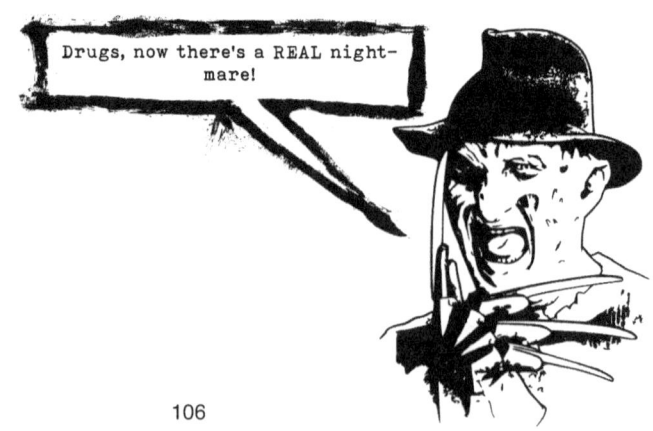

Drugs, now there's a REAL nightmare!

"Dust to Dust"

Original Air Date: Sunday, February 25, 1990
Season 2, Episode 20

Director: Bill Froelich

Writers: David Braff, Bill Froelich, Jonathan Glassner

Cast: Tony Dow, Sandahl Bergman, Amy Lyndon, Martha Smith, Tim Russ, Richard Brestoff, Oliver Bodnar, Janet Keyser, Greg Wrangler, Robert Englund

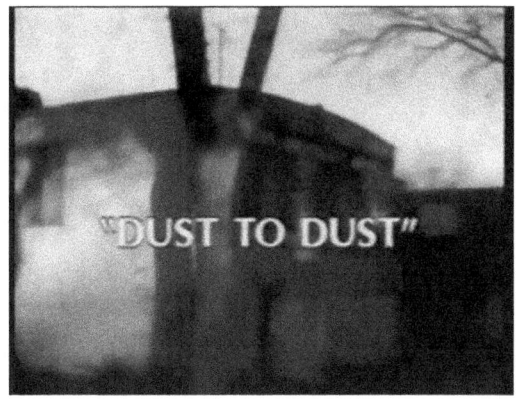

Synopsis

A Story - Johnny, Mary Beth and Ginger are recovering from their plane crash ordeal that left them with no option but to eat their dead friends. When a man charges into their home and attacks Johnny, the ladies come to his rescue and dispatch the intruder. The group needs to dispose of the evidence and they can see only one option.

B Story - Johnny, Mary Beth and Ginger are taken to a secret facility after it is discovered that the man that they ate was an astronaut who was infected with a mysterious virus. Johnny is infected and the ladies are in the clear, but they already know too much and the scientists are determined to continue their experiments.

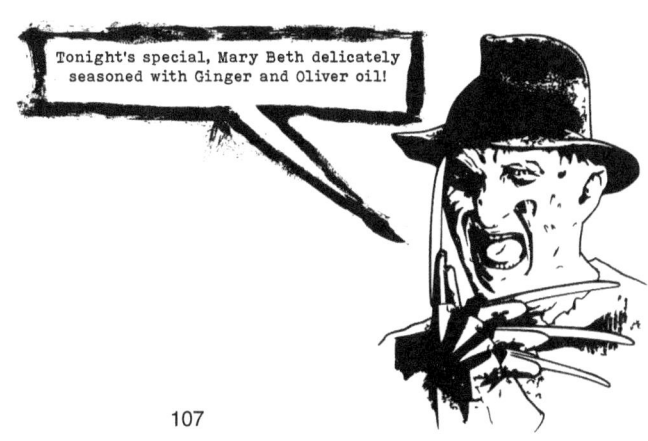

Tonight's special, Mary Beth delicately seasoned with Ginger and Oliver oil!

107

"Prisoner of Love"

Original Air Date: Sunday, March 4, 1990
Season 2, Episode 21

Director: Richard T. Schor

Writers: Richard Beban

Cast: Vincent Baggetta, Maria Richwine, Tara Buckman, John Milford, Serina Grant, Gabor Morea, Biff Yeager, Robert Englund

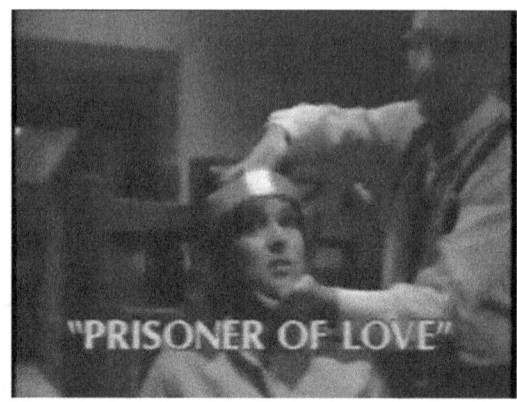

Synopsis

A Story - Reverend Jarvis is at Springwood Prison to administer the last rites to Violet, a death row inmate. When Jarvis begins to fall for Violet the two hatch an elaborate scheme to break her out of prison, but when things don't go according to plan Violet finds herself trapped in a different kind of prison.

B Story - Brenda, an inmate at Springwood Prison knows a secret that Reverend Jarvis wants to keep buried and he will go to great lengths to keep it that way.

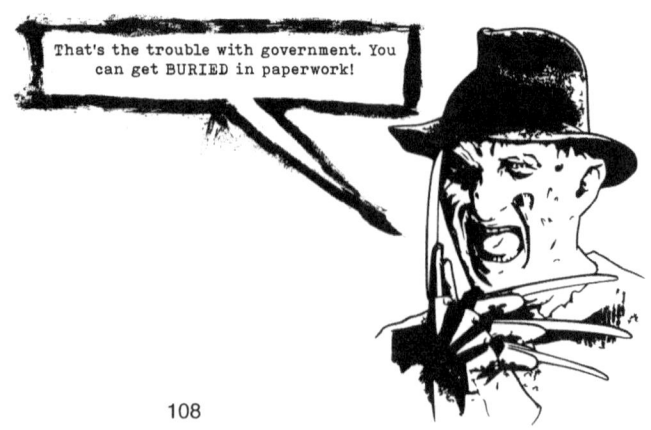

That's the trouble with government. You can get BURIED in paperwork!

"Life Sentence"

Original Air Date: Sunday, March 11, 1990
Season 2, Episode 22

Director: Anita W. Addison

Writers: David Zuckerman

Cast: George de la Pena, Penny Johnson, Glynn Turman, Ron Troncatty, John Milford, Ray Cruz, Otto Coelho, Jolina Mitchell, Robert Englund

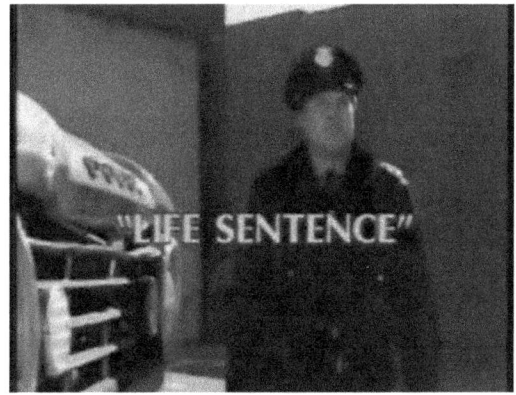

Synopsis

A Story - Andy is up for parole at Springwood Prison but must first be cleared by Elaine, the new prison psychiatrist. Andy soon finds out that Elaine has anterior motives for keeping him locked up behind bars.

B Story - Warden Hendler is running for office and is behind in the polls. Hendler resorts to using an experimental drug to extract information from inmate Andy for his own personal gain. When Andy dies during the experiment, Hendler must cover his tracks, but is this a secret that he will be able to keep?

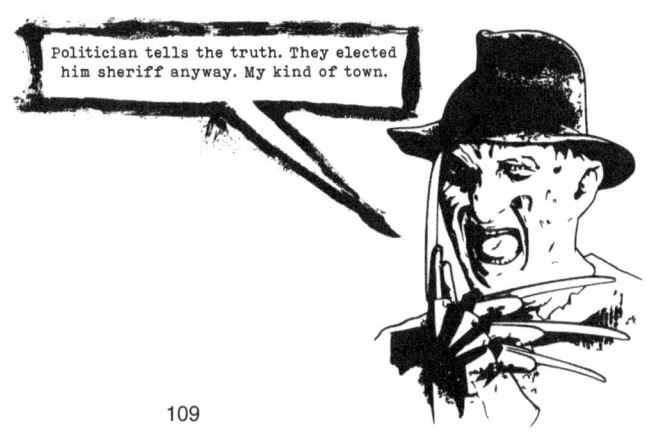

Politician tells the truth. They elected him sheriff anyway. My kind of town.

APPENDICES

Appendix A: Selection of Notable Anthology Series (1955-1990)
Appendix B: *Freddy's Nightmares* Directors
Appendix C: *Freddy's Nightmares* Directors Selected Filmographies
Appendix D: *Freddy's Nightmares* Writers
Appendix E: Episode Connections
Appendix F: Selected International Home Video Releases
Appendix G: Season One Press Kit [29]
Appendix H: Season Two Press Kit [30]
Appendix I: Lorimar Promotional Stills [31]

Appendix A

Selection of Notable Anthology Series (1955-1990)

Title	Year	Seasons
Alfred Hitchcock Presents	1955	10
The Twilight Zone	1959	5
Thriller	1960	2
The Outer Limits	1963	2
Mystery and Imagination	1966	5
Night Gallery	1969	3
Thriller	1973	6
Darkroom	1981	2
The Hitchhiker	1983	6
Tales from the Darkside	1983	4
Amazing Stories	1985	2
Alfred Hitchcock Presents	1985	4
The Twilight Zone	1985	3
Ray Bradbury Theatre	1985	6
Freddy's Nightmares	1988	2
Monsters	1988	3
Tales from the Crypt	1989	7
Are You Afraid of the Dark?	1990	10

Appendix B

Freddy's Nightmares Directors

Director	Episodes
Tobe Hooper	S01E01
Tom McLoughlin	S01E02
Mick Garris	S01E03
Ken Wiederhorn	S01E04, S01E07, S01E18, S02E03, S02E13, S02E16, S02E17
Tom DeSimone	S01E05, S02E04, S02E11, S02E12
Lisa Gottlieb	S01E06
Michael Lange	S01E08, S01E13
John Lafia	S01E09, S01E17
George Kaczender	S01E10, S01E14, S02E01
Dwight Little	S01E11
Jonathan Betuel	S01E12, S01E20
Michael Klein	S01E15
Robert Englund	S01E16, S02E09
Jeff Freilich	S01E19
David K. Calloway	S01E21, S02E15
Jerry Olson	S01E22
William Malone	S02E02, S02E06, S02E14
Don Weis	S02E05
Chuck Braverman	S02E07
James Quinn	S02E08
Bill Froelich	S02E10, S02E20
Gilbert Adler	S02E18
Keith Samples	S02E19
Richard T. Schor	S02E21
Anita W. Addison	S02E22

Appendix C

Anita Addison Selected Directorial Filmography

Freddy's Nightmares	1 Episode	1990
Knot's Landing	2 Episodes	1990-1991
Sisters	1 Episode	1991
Homefront	1 Episode	1992
Quantum Leap	2 Episodes	1991-1992
Sirens	Movie	1993
There are No Children Here	Movie	1993
ER	1 Episode	1995
The Great Defender	1 Episode	1995
EZ Streets	1 Episode	1997
Deep in my Heart	Movie	1999
Judging Amy	1 Episode	2000
Copshop	Movie	2004

Gilbert Adler Selected Directorial Filmography

Freddy's Nightmares	1 Episode	1990
Tales from the Crypt	2 Episodes	1992-1993
Bordello of Blood	Movie	1996
Perversions of Science	1 Episode	1996
Fantasy Island	1 Episode	1998
Charmed	1 Episode	1998

Jonathan Betuel Selected Directorial Filmography

My Science Project	Movie	1985
CBS Summer Playhouse	1 Episode	1988
Freddy's Nightmares	2 Episodes	1989
Theodore Rex	Movie	1995

Chuck Braverman Selected Directorial Filmography

The Horror Hall of Fame	Movie	1974
The Making of 'Beatlemania'	Movie	1978
Prince of Bel Air	Movie	1986
The Brotherhood of Justice	Movie	1986
Rags to Riches	1 Episode	1987
Sledge Hammer!	6 Episodes	1986-1987
Freddy's Nightmares	1 Episode	1989
Life Goes On	1 Episode	1990
Beverly Hills, 90210	9 Episodes	1991
Northern Exposure	1 Episode	1992
Melrose Place	2 Episodes	1992
Baywatch	1 Episode	1994
Hercules: The Legendary Journeys	1 Episode	1996
Season of the Grizzly	Movie	2003
The Secret Tapes of the OJ Case	Movie	2015

David K. Calloway Selected Directorial Filmography

Freddy's Nightmares	2 Episodes	1989-1990
Dark Justice	10 Episodes	1991-1993
She Spies	1 Episode	2003

Tom DeSimone Selected Directorial Filmography

Chatterbox!	Movie	1977
The Dirty Picture Show	Movie	1980
Hell Night	Movie	1981
The Concrete Jungle	Movie	1982
Savage Streets (Uncredited)	Movie	1984
Hellhole (Uncredited)	Movie	1985
Reform School Girls	Movie	1986
Angel III: The Final Chapter	Movie	1988
Freddy's Nightmares	4 Episodes	1988-1989
Super Force	9 Episodes	1991-1992
Swamp Thing	3 Episodes	1992-1993
Dark Justice	7 Episodes	1991-1993
The Big Easy	4 Episodes	1996-1997
She Spies	1 Episode	2002

Robert Englund Selected Directorial Filmography

976-EVIL	Movie	1988
Freddy's Nightmares	2 Episodes	1989
Killer Pad	Movie	2008

Jeff Freilich Selected Directorial Filmography

Falcon Crest	6 Episodes	1987-1988
Freddy's Nightmares	1 Episode	1989
Dark Justice	9 Episodes	1991-1993
Naked City: Justice with a Bullet	Movie	1998
Code Name Phoenix	Movie	2000
Burn Notice	2 Episodes	2008-2009
Halt and Catch Fire	3 Episodes	2015-2017

Bill Froelich Selected Directorial Filmography

Return to Horror High	Movie	1987
A Fine Romance	1 Episode	1989
Freddy's Nightmares	2 Episodes	1989-1990
Rogue Waves	Movie	2006

Mick Garris Selected Directorial Filmography

Amazing Stories	1 Episode	1986
Critters 2: The Main Course	Movie	1988
Freddy's Nightmares	1 Episode	1988
Psycho IV: The Beginning	Movie	1990
Sleepwalkers	Movie	1992
The Stand	Movie	1994
Tales from the Crypt	1 Episode	1994
Quicksilver Highway	Movie	1997
The Shining	Movie	1997
Riding the Bullet	Movie	2004
Desperation	Movie	2006
Masters of Horror	2 Episodes	2005-2006
Bag of Bones	Movie	2011
Nightmare Cinema	Movie	2018

Lisa Gottlieb Selected Directorial Filmography

Just One of the Guys	Movie	1985
Freddy's Nightmares	1 Episode	1988
Dream On	1 Episode	1994
Across the Moon	Movie	1994
Cadillac Ranch	Movie	1996
Boy Meets World	1 Episode	1998

Tobe Hooper Selected Directorial Filmography

Eggshells	Movie	1969
The Texas Chainsaw Massacre	Movie	1974
Eaten Alive	Movie	1976
Salem's Lot	Movie	1979
The Funhouse	Movie	1981
Poltergeist	Movie	1982
Lifeforce	Movie	1985
Invaders from Mars	Movie	1986
The Texas Chainsaw Massacre 2	Movie	1986
Amazing Stories	1 Episode	1987
Freddy's Nightmares	1 Episode	1988
Spontaneous Combustion	Movie	1989
Tales from the Crypt	1 Episode	1991
Night Terrors	Movie	1993
The Mangler	Movie	1995
Toolbox Murders	Movie	2004
Mortuary	Movie	2005
Masters of Horror	2 Episodes	2005-2006
Djinn	Movie	2013

George Kaczender Selected Directorial Filmography

Don't Let the Angels Fall	Movie	1969
The Girl in Blue	Movie	1973
In Praise of Older Women	Movie	1978
The Agency	Movie	1980
Tomorrow's a Killer	Movie	1987
Night Heat	7 Episodes	1985-1988
Falcon Crest	3 Episodes	1988
Freddy's Nightmares	3 Episodes	1988-1989
A Seduction in Travis County	Movie	1991
Betrayal of Trust	Movie	1994
Maternal Instincts	Movie	1996

Michael Klein Selected Directorial Filmography

Nine to Five	2 Episodes	1987-1988
She's the Sheriff	1 Episode	1988
Freddy's Nightmares	1 Episode	1989

John Lafia Selected Directorial Filmography

The Blue Iguana	Movie	1988
Freddy's Nightmares	2 Episodes	1988-1989
Monsters	1 Episode	1989
Child's Play 2	Movie	1990
Dark Justice	2 Episodes	1991
Man's Best Friend	Movie	1993
Babylon 5	3 Episodes	1997
The Dead Zone	1 Episode	2002
The Rats	Movie	2002
10.5	Movie	2004
10.5: Apocalypse	Movie	2006
Firestorm: Last Stand at Yellowstone	Movie	2006

Michael Lange Selected Directorial Filmography

T.J. Hooker	1 Episode	1985
Riptide	9 Episodes	1984-1986
Rags to Riches	3 Episodes	1987-1988
Freddy's Nightmares	2 Episodes	1988-1989
Dynasty	1 Episode	1989
Jake and the Fatman	8 Episodes	1987-1991
Knot's Landing	2 Episodes	1991-1992
Life Goes On	16 Episodes	1991-1993
Adventures of Brisco County, Jr.	1 Episode	1993
Northern Exposure	5 Episodes	1993-1995
Weird Science	2 Episodes	1996
The X-Files	4 Episodes	1994-1997
Hercules: The Legendary Journeys	2 Episodes	1996-1997
Buffy the Vampire Slayer	4 Episodes	1998-1999
Beverly Hills, 90210	13 Episodes	1994-2000
Dawson's Creek	7 Episodes	2000-2003
The O.C.	13 Episodes	2003-2006
Eureka	4 Episodes	2006-2007
Criminal Minds	5 Episodes	2012-2013
Bones	7 Episodes	2014-2017
Charmed	1 Episode	2018
Cowboy Drifter	Movie	2022

Dwight Little Selected Directorial Filmography

KGB: The Secret War	Movie	1985
Getting Even	Movie	1986
Bloodstone	Movie	1988
Halloween 4	Movie	1988
Freddy's Nightmares	1 Episode	1989
Phantom of the Opera	Movie	1989
Marked for Death	Movie	1990
Rapid Fire	Movie	1992
Free Willy 2: The Adventure Home	Movie	1995
Murder at 1600	Movie	1997
Millenium	3 Episodes	1997-1999
Boss of Bosses	Movie	2001
The X-Files	1 Episode	2002
The Practice	9 Episodes	1998-2002
Anacondas: Hunt for the Blood Orchid	Movie	2004
24	2 Episodes	2006
Prison Break	5 Episodes	2005-2009
Dollhouse	1 Episode	2009
Tekken	Movie	2010
Nikita	5 Episodes	2011-2013
From Dusk til Dawn: The Series	4 Episodes	2014-2016
Bones	23 Episodes	2006-2017

William Malone Selected Directorial Filmography

Scared to Death	Movie	1980
Creature	Movie	1985
Freddy's Nightmares	3 Episodes	1989-1990
Dark Justice	3 Episodes	1993
Tales from the Crypt	2 Episodes	1994-1996
The Big Easy	3 Episodes	1997
House on Haunted Hill	Movie	1999
Feardotcom	Movie	2002
Masters of Horror	1 Episode	2006
Parasomnia	Movie	2008

Tom McLoughlin Selected Directorial Filmography

One Dark Night	Movie	1982
Friday the 13th: Jason Lives	Movie	1986
Date with an Angel	Movie	1987
Freddy's Nightmares	1 Episode	1988
Friday the 13th: The Series	4 Episodes	1988-1989
Sometimes They Come Back	Movie	1991
Murder of Innocence	Movie	1993

Jerry Olson Selected Directorial Filmography

Freddy's Nightmares	1 Episode	1989
Queen of Hearts	Movie	2019

James Quinn Selected Directorial Filmography

Miami Vice	3 Episodes	1987
Crime Story	2 Episodes	1987
Freddy's Nightmares	1 Episode	1989
Midnight Caller	8 Episodes	1989-1991
Blind Man's Bluff	Movie	1992
The Untouchables	4 Episodes	1993-1994
Profiler	3 Episodes	1998-2000
Early Edition	6 Episodes	1997-2000
Law and Order: SVU	2 Episodes	2001
Law and Order	11 Episodes	1990-2003

Keith Samples Selected Directorial Filmography

Freddy's Nightmares	1 Episode	1990
A Smile Like Yours	Movie	1997
OZ	3 Episodes	1998-2000
The Practice	3 Episodes	1999-2001
Dawson's Creek	2 Episodes	2001-2002
Felicity	6 Episodes	1999-2002
Single White Female 2: The Psycho	Movie	2005
Republic of Doyle	7 Episodes	2011-2012
Mr. D	23 Episodes	2012-2018

Richard T. Schor Selected Directorial Filmography

Freddy's Nightmares	1 Episode	1990

Don Weis Selected Directorial Filmography

The Affair of Dobie Gillis	Movie	1953
Dear Phoebe	5 Episodes	1954
The Thin Man	14 Episodes	1958-1959
The Andy Griffith Show	9 Episodes	1960
Alfred Hitchcock Presents	5 Episodes	1955-1962
The Twilight Zone	1 Episode	1963
Perry Mason	1 Episode	1963
Burke's Law	13 Episodes	1963-1965
The Patty Duke Show	9 Episodes	1964-1965
The Ghost in the Invisible Bikini	Movie	1966
Batman	4 Episodes	1966
It Takes a Thief	13 Episodes	1968-1969
Happy Days	1 Episode	1974
Planet of the Apes	4 Episodes	1974
Kolchak: The Night Stalker	4 Episodes	1974-1975
Starsky and Hutch	7 Episodes	1975-1977
M*A*S*H	16 Episodes	1972-1978
Hawaii Five-O	11 Episodes	1977-1980
CHiPs	9 Episodes	1979-1980
Fantasy Island	22 Episodes	1978-1984
The Love Boat	7 Episodes	1977-1984
Remington Steele	17 Episodes	1983-1986
MacGyver	1 Episode	1986
Freddy's Nightmares	1 Episode	1989

Ken Wiederhorn Selected Directorial Filmography

Shock Waves	Movie	1977
King Frat	Movie	1979
Eyes of a Stranger	Movie	1981
Meatballs Part II	Movie	1984
Return of the Living Dead II	Movie	1988
Freddy's Nightmares	7 Episodes	1988-1990
21 Jump Street	2 Episodes	1989-1990
Dark Justice	6 Episodes	1991-1992
A House in the Hills	Movie	1993

Appendix D

Freddy's Nightmares Writers

S01E01	"No More Mr. Nice Guy"	Rhet Topham, Michael DeLuca, David Erhman
S01E02	"It's a Miserable Life"	Michael DeLuca, Paul Rosselli
S01E03	"Killer Instinct"	Alan B. Ury
S01E04	"Freddy's Tricks and Treats"	Alan Katz, Gil Adler
S01E05	"Judy Miller, Come on Down"	Jack Temchin, Michael DeLuca
S01E06	"Saturday Night Special"	Don Bohlinger, James Nathan
S01E07	"Sister's Keeper"	Michael DeLuca, Jeff Freilich
S01E08	"Mother's Day"	David Ehrman
S01E09	"Rebel Without a Car"	Christopher Trumbo
S01E10	"The Bride Wore Red"	Howard Lakin
S01E11	"Do Dreams Bleed"	Michael DeLuca
S01E12	"The End of the World"	James Cappe
S01E13	"Deadline"	Jill Donner
S01E14	"Black Tickets"	Howard Lakin
S01E15	"School Daze"	David Ehrman
S01E16	"Cabin Fever"	Rhet Topham
S01E17	"Love Stinks"	Michael DeLuca, Jeff Freilich
S01E18	"The Art of Death"	Michael DeLuca, Ken Wiederhorn
S01E19	"Missing Persons"	Jeff Freilich
S01E20	"The Light at the End of the Tunnel"	James Cappe, Jonathan Betuel
S01E21	"Identity Crisis"	Rebecca Pogrow
S01E22	"Safe Sex"	David J. Schow
S02E01	"Dream Come True"	Tom Blomquist, Tom Lazarus
S02E02	"Heartbreak Hotel"	Jonathan Glassner
S02E03	"Welcome to Springwood"	Alan Katz, Gil Adler
S02E04	"Photo Finish"	Bill Froelich
S02E05	"Memory Overload"	Michael Kirschenbaum
S02E06	"Lucky Stiff"	David Braff
S02E07	"Silence is Golden"	Jonathan Glassner
S02E08	"Bloodlines"	Alan Katz, Gil Adler
S02E09	"Monkey Dreams"	Michael Kirschenbaum
S02E10	"Do You Know Where Your Kids Are?"	Wayne Allan Rice
S02E11	"Dreams that Kill"	Tom Blomquist
S02E12	"It's My Party and You'll Die if I Want You To"	David Braff
S02E13	"What You Don't Know Can Kill You"	Jonathan Glassner
S02E14	"Easy Come, Easy Go"	David Braff
S02E15	"Prime Cut"	Michael Kirschenbaum
S02E16	"Interior Loft"	David Braff
S02E17	"Interior Loft Later"	Jonathan Glassner
S02E18	"Funhouse"	Gil Adler
S02E19	"A Family Affair"	David Braff
S02E20	"Dust to Dust"	David Braff
S02E21	"Prisoner of Love"	Richard Beban
S02E22	"Life Sentence"	David Zuckerman

Appendix E

<u>Episode Connections</u>

Many episodes, mostly from season two, featured connected storylines so that two episodes could be edited into a feature length film for foreign distribution.

"No More Mr. Nice Guy" → "Sister's Keeper"

"Memory Overload" → "Monkey Dreams"

"Bloodlines" → "Do You Know Where Your Kids Are?"

"Dream Come True" → "Dreams That Kill"

"Lucky Stiff" → "Easy Come, Easy Go"

"Prime Cut" → "Dust To Dust"

"Photo Finish" → "It's My Party And You'll Die If I Want You To"

"Interior Loft" → "Interior Loft Later"

"Welcome To Springwood" → "Funhouse"

"Silence Is Golden" → "A Family Affair"

"Prisoner Of Love" → "Life Sentence"

Selected International Home Video Releases

United States:

1. "No More Mr. Nice Guy"
2. "Freddy's Tricks And Treats"
3. "Lucky Stiff"
4. "Dreams That Kill"
5. "It's My Party And You'll Die If I Want You To"

United Kingdom:

1. ***The Nightmare Begins Again***
   - "No More Mr. Nice Guy"
   - "Killer Instinct"
2. ***Freddy's Nightmares Part 2***
   - "Sister's Keeper"
   - "Freddy's Tricks And Treats"
3. ***Rock Me Freddy***
   - "Judy Miller, Come On Down"
   - "The Bride Wore Red"
4. ***Saturday Nightmare Fever***
   - "Saturday Night Special"
   - "Cabin Fever"
5. ***Do Dreams Bleed***
   - "Do Dreams Bleed"
   - "Rebel Without A Car"
6. ***Freddy's Mother's Day***
   - "Mother's Day"
   - "Black Tickets"
7. ***Safe Sex***
   - "Safe Sex"
   - "Deadline"
8. ***It's A Miserable Life***
   - "It's A Miserable Life"
   - "Love Stinks"

Japan:

1. "No More Mr. Nice Guy," "It's A Miserable Life"
2. "Killer Instinct," "Freddy's Tricks And Treats"
3. "Saturday Night Special," "Judy Miller, Come On Down"
4. "Mother's Day," "Sister's Keeper"
5. "Rebel Without A Car," "The Bride Wore Red"
6. "Do Dreams Bleed," "Out To Lunch*"
7. "Deadline," "Black Tickets"
8. "School Daze," "Cabin Fever"

*"The End of the World" was retitled for the Japanese home video release

Australia:

1. "It's A Miserable Life," "Freddy's Tricks And Treats"
2. "Deadline," "Black Tickets"
3. "Love Stinks," "Judy Miller, Come On Down"
4. "Rebel Without A Car," "The Bride Wore Red"
5. "Do Dreams Bleed," "The End of the World"
6. "No More Mr. Nice Guy," "Killer Instinct"
7. "School Daze," "Cabin Fever"
8. "Mother's Day," "Sister's Keeper"

Freddy's Nightmares

A Nightmare

ON ELM STREET:
THE SERIES

Show Description

It's hard to keep a bad man down. And so it goes with Freddy Krueger, one of the most terrifying characters in film history. Now, Freddy brings his macabre mixture of humor and horror to television with the new syndicated weekly one-hour episodic series "Freddy's Nightmares," based on the blockbuster feature film series "A Nightmare on Elm Street." Robert Englund, reprising his popular role of the monstrous, wisecracking Freddy Kreuger, serves as host and frequent cast member.

As was revealed in the original 1984 "A Nightmare on Elm Street," Freddy met a fiery death at the hands of vengeful Springwood parents, who took the law into their own hands after the judicial system failed to put away the teen-murdering janitor. After his "death," the grossly disfigured Freddy returned as something far worse, a dream demon capable of invading and exploiting people's deepest, darkest thoughts and nightmares. When the film, which cost $1.8 million, wound up earning $24 million, producer Robert Shaye realized that what had started out to be just "a nice little horror film" had become a cult phenomenon, and so Freddy was revived for a second, a third and recently, a fourth motion picture.

"A Nightmare on Elm Street," the television series, explores the eerie nether world of Freddy Krueger and his revenge on the citizens of Springwood, where dreams become reality and reality turns into horrifying nightmares. Unlike your normal breed of middle

-more-

A Stone Television production in association with New Line Cinema, distributed by Lorimar Syndication
10202 West Washington Boulevard • Culver City, CA 90232 • (213) 280-2210

**"A NIGHTMARE ON ELM STREET - FREDDY'S NIGHTMARES:
THE SERIES"**
Show Description

Americans, the denizens of Springwood are haunted by their thoughts, hopes, wishes, and daydreams. In his trademark tattered sweater, felt fedora hat and razor-fingered glove, Freddy and his minions ride herd over Springwood's subconscious, decimating its citizens with a psychologically terrifying edge.

"Freddy's Nightmares" will feature 22 one-hour episodes, each of which will contain two separate stories. You'll never know when "host" Freddy will pop up with his evil smirk and strikingly sardonic humor to preside over the festivities. The series delves into the horror-fantasy side of our subconscious with sometimes darkly humorous consequences. For example, the gruesome price of winning when a track star is urged to get the "killer instinct;" the chilling side-effects of a young woman's repressed sexuality; and the nightmare of being Freddy's patient at Springwood's hospital. The series also exploits the simple apprehensions of everyday life: the gnawing guilt of adultery; the fear of discovery; the dread of the dentist's chair; and the ever-present perils of dating in the '80's.

With his razor-sharp wit, Freddy is the man of our dreams, the hero that people love to hate. He will lure us into a world where our dark side is exposed while he zeroes in for the kill in his quest for fiendish fun.

"Freddy's Nightmares" will also feature the talents of motion picture directors Tobe Hooper ("Poltergeist" and "The Texas Chainsaw Massacre"), Mick Garris ("Critters 2"), Renny Harlan ("A Nightmare on Elm Street, Part 4") and Tim Hunter ("River's Edge"). "A Nightmare on Elm Street: Freddy's Nightmares" is a Stone Television production in association with New Line Cinema distributed by Lorimar Syndication. Robert Shaye and Jeff Freilich are executive producers.

# # #

Contact: David Stapf   FREDPK
           (213) 280-2217

Freddy's Nightmares

A Nightmare

ON ELM STREET:
THE SERIES

"A NIGHTMARE ON ELM STREET - FREDDY'S NIGHTMARES:
THE SERIES

The following are cast and production credits for **"A Nightmare on Elm Street - Freddy's Nightmares: The Series,"** the one-hour suspense series for first-run syndication.

Origination:	Filmed in and around Los Angeles, CA
Format:	One-hour Suspense Drama
Host:	**ROBERT ENGLUND as Freddy Krueger**
Executive Producers:	Robert Shaye Jeff Freilich
Executive in charge of Production:	Scott Stone
Producer:	Gil Adler
Supervising Producer:	Jonathan Betuel
Production Designer:	Mick Strawn
Editors:	Arthur Klein Phil Scriccia
Press Representative:	David Stapf (213) 280-2217

# # #

FNFYI

A Stone Television production in association with New Line Cinema, distributed by Lorimar Syndication
10202 West Washington Boulevard • Culver City, CA 90232 • (213) 280-2210

127

Freddy's Nightmares

A Nightmare
ON ELM STREET:
THE SERIES

ROBERT ENGLUND
(Freddy Krueger)

Robert Englund, best known to audiences as the sinister Freddy Krueger in the "A Nightmare on Elm Street" blockbuster series of feature films, was born on June 6 in Los Angeles, CA. The only son of non-show business parents (his engineer father helped develop the infamous U-2 spy plane), Englund's interest in the arts began while attending college at California State University, Northridge as well as UCLA.

He went on to study acting with such renowned acting coaches as Lee Strasberg, Jeff Corey and Jack Garfein and graduated with honors from the American branch of the Royal Academy of Dramatic Arts. After acting and directing in theatres around the country and managing a theatre in Los Angeles, Englund made the transition to film with a role in the 1974 feature "Buster and Billie." He went on to star in "Hustle," "Stay Hungry," "A Star is Born," "Big Wednesday," "Don't Cry, It's Only Thunder," "The Quest" and beginning in 1984, the "Freddy" sagas: "A Nightmare on Elm Street," "A Nightmare on Elm Street II," "A Nightmare on Elm Street III: Dream Warriors" and the recently released "A Nightmare on Elm Street IV: The Dream Master."

Englund is also a prolific television actor, having starred in such telefilms as "Young Joe, The Forgotten Kennedy," "Get Patty Hearst," "Hobson's Choice," "I Want to Live" and "Starflight One."

-more-

A Stone Television production in association with New Line Cinema, distributed by Lorimar Syndication
10202 West Washington Boulevard • Culver City, CA 90232 • (213) 280-2210

Englund also starred in the television series "Downtown" and reprised his role as the gentle lizard Willy from the mini-series "V" in the weekly series of the same name. He makes his feature film directorial debut in the upcoming motion picture "976-EVIL."

# # #

Contact: David Stapf   RER
            (213) 280-2217

Freddy's Nightmares
A Nightmare

ON ELM STREET:
THE SERIES

ROBERT SHAYE
(Executive Producer)

Since founding New Line Cinema in 1967, Robert Shaye has served as President and Chief Executive Officer where he has overseen the acquisition and marketing of such popular releases as "Sympathy for the Devil," "The Seduction of Mimi," the re-release of the cult hit "The Texas Chainsaw Massacre" and the 1978 Academy Award winner for Best Foreign Film, "Get Out Your Handkerchiefs." He has also served as executive producer for New Line on the feature films "Stunts," "Alone in the Dark," "The First Time," "Xtro," "Polyester," "Critters," "Quiet Cool" and the four "Nightmare on Elm Street" films. Prior to founding New Line, he produced and directed such award-winning short films as "Image" and "On Fighting Witches."

Shaye received a B.B.A. degree from the University of Michigan School of Business Administration and an L.L.B. from Columbia Law School. Selected as a Fullbright Scholar in the field of copyright law, he is currently a member of the state of New York Bar Association.

# # #

Contact: David Stapf
           (213) 280-2217

FREDRSBIO

A Stone Television production in association with New Line Cinema, distributed by Lorimar Syndication
10202 West Washington Boulevard • Culver City, CA 90232 • (213) 280-2210

Freddys Nightmares

A Nightmare
ON ELM STREET:
THE SERIES

JEFF FREILICH
(Executive Producer)

Jeff Freilich, a 1970 production graduate of the renowned American Film Institute, began his show business career at Universal Television where he served as a creative consultant on "Baretta." He subsequently served as executive story consultant on the series "Quincy" and produced both "The Incredible Hulk" and "Galactica 1980."

In 1980, Freilich joined Lorimar as executive story editor for the nighttime drama "Flamingo Road." He went on to be supervising producer of the series "Boone," co-creator and executive producer of "Better Days" and most recently, served as executive producer of "Falcon Crest" for the past two television seasons.

Freilich's feature film credits include screenwriting credits on "Two Scoops," "Hollywood Boulevard," "Paradise Flats," "Outta Sight," "Patrolwomen" and "Dynamite."

A 1969 graduate of Antioch College, Freilich resides in Los Angeles, CA.

# # #

Contact: David Stapf   FREDJFBIO
           (213) 280-2217

A Stone Television production in association with New Line Cinema, distributed by Lorimar Syndication
10202 West Washington Boulevard • Culver City, CA 90232 • (213) 280-2210

Freddys Nightmares

A Nightmare

ON ELM STREET:
THE SERIES

"A NIGHTMARE ON ELM STREET- FREDDY'S NIGHTMARES: THE SERIES"
COLOR CAPTIONS

Slide A: Robert Englund stars as the sinister, razor-fingered Freddy Krueger in "A Nightmare on Elm Street - Freddy's Nightmares: The Series."

Slide B: Robert Englund reprises his role as the grossly disfigured Freddy Krueger from the blockbuster "A Nightmare on Elm Street" films in the new one-hour suspense television series "A Nightmare on Elm Street - Freddy's Nightmares: The Series."

Slide C: Robert Englund serves as host and frequent cast member Freddy Krueger in "A Nightmare on Elm Street - Freddy's Nightmares: The Series."

Slide D: Robert Englund stars as the debonair demon of the dark, Freddy Krueger, in "A Nightmare on Elm Street - Freddy's Nightmares: The Series."

# # #

Contact: David Stapf   FNCOLOR88
(213) 280-2217

A Stone Television production in association with New Line Cinema, distributed by Lorimar Syndication
10202 West Washington Boulevard • Culver City, CA 90232 • (213) 280-2210

LORIMAR

NEWS RELEASE

September 22, 1988

Dear Television Editor/Writer:

Please note that the correct title of the series is --

"A NIGHTMARE ON ELM STREET - FREDDY'S NIGHTMARES: THE SERIES."

Thank you,

David Stapf
(213) 280-2217

Season Two Press Kit

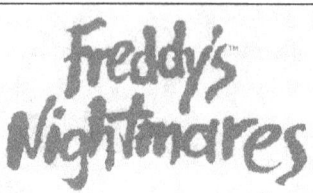

The following are cast and production credits for "Freddy's Nightmares," the one-hour suspense series for first-run syndication.

Origination:	Filmed in and around Los Angeles, CA
Format:	One-hour Suspense Drama
Host:	**ROBERT ENGLUND as Freddy Krueger**
Executive Producers:	Robert Shaye Scott Stone
Producer:	Gil Adler
Production Designer:	Greg Melton
Press Representative:	Paul Gendreau (213) 280-2214

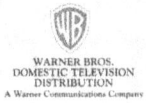

WARNER BROS.
DOMESTIC TELEVISION
DISTRIBUTION
A Warner Communications Company

1989-'90 SHOW DESCRIPTION

It's hard to keep a bad man down. And so it goes with Freddy Krueger, one of the most terrifying characters in film history. Now, Freddy's macabre mixture of humor and horror returns to television for a second season with the syndicated weekly one-hour episodic series "Freddy's Nightmares," based on the blockbuster feature film series "A Nightmare on Elm Street." Robert Englund, reprising his popular role of the monstrous, wisecracking Freddy Krueger, serves as host and frequent cast member.

As was revealed in the original 1984 "A Nightmare on Elm Street," Freddy met a fiery death at the hands of vengeful Springwood parents, who took the law into their own hands after the judicial system failed to put away the teen-murdering janitor. After his death, the grossly disfigured Freddy returned as something far worse, a dream demon capable of invading and exploiting people's deepest, darkest thoughts and nightmares. When the film, which cost $1.8 million, wound up earning $24 million, producer Robert Shaye realized that what had started out to be just "a nice little horror film" had become a cult phenomenon, and so Freddy was revived for a second, a third, a fourth, and recently, a fifth motion picture.

"Freddy's Nightmares" explores the eerie nether world of Freddy Krueger and his revenge on the citizens of Springwood, where dreams become reality and reality turns into horrifying nightmares. Unlike your normal breed of middle Americans, the denizens of Springwood are haunted by their thoughts, hopes, wishes, and daydreams. In his trademark tattered sweater, felt fedora hat and razor-fingered glove, Freddy and his minions ride herd over Springwood's subconscious, decimating its citizens with a psychologically terrifying edge.

"Freddy's Nightmares" will again feature 22 original one-hour episodes this season, each of which will contain two separate stories. You'll never know when "host" Freddy will pop up with his evil smirk and strikingly sardonic humor to preside over the festivities. The series delves into the horror-fantasy side of the human subconscious with sometimes darkly humorous consequences. The series also exploits the simple apprehensions of everyday life: the gnawing guilt of adultery; the fear of discovery; the dread of the dentist's chair; and the ever-present perils of dating in the 80's.

With his razor-sharp wit, Freddy is the man of our dreams, the hero that people love to hate. He will lure us into a world where our dark side is exposed while he zeroes in for the kill in his quest for fiendish fun.

"Freddy's Nightmares" is a Stone Television production in association with New Line Cinema, and is distributed by Warner Bros. Domestic Television Distribution. Robert Shaye and Scott Stone are executive producers.

Contact: Paul Gendreau
(213) 280-2214

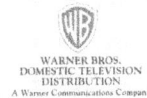

WARNER BROS.
DOMESTIC TELEVISION
DISTRIBUTION
A Warner Communications Company

ROBERT ENGLUND
(Freddy Krueger)

Robert Englund, best known to audiences as the sinister Freddy Krueger in the "A Nightmare on Elm Street" blockbuster series of feature films, was born on June 6 in Los Angeles, CA. The only son of non-show business parents (his engineer father helped develop the infamous U-2 spy plane), Englund's interest in the arts began while attending college at California State University, Northridge as well as UCLA.

He went on to study acting with such renowned acting coaches as Lee Strasberg, Jeff Corey and Jack Garfein and graduated with honors from the American branch of the Royal Academy of Dramatic Arts. After acting and directing in theatres around the country and managing a theatre in Los Angeles, Englund made the transition to film with a role in the 1974 feature "Buster and Billie." He went on to star in "Hustle," "Stay Hungry," "A Star is Born," "Big Wednesday," "Don't Cry, It's Only Thunder," "The Quest" and beginning in 1984, the "Freddy" sagas: "A Nightmare on Elm Street," "A Nightmare on Elm Street II," "A Nightmare on Elm Street III: Dream Warriors," "A Nightmare on Elm Street IV: The Dream Master," and the recently released "A Nightmare on Elm Street V: The Dream Child."

Englund is also a prolific television actor, having starred in such telefilms as "Young Joe, The Forgotten Kennedy," "Get Patty Hearst," "Hobson's Choice," "I Want to Live," "Starflight One," the television series "Downtown" and in the mini-series "V;" in the weekly series of the same name, he repeated his role of the gentle lizard Willy. Englund made his feature film directorial debut this past year with the motion picture "976-EVIL."

Busier than ever, Englund recently completed filming in Europe for the feature film "The Phantom of the Opera," in which he stars as the tragic title character. In addition, he is currently filming another feature film, "Ford Fairlane," scheduled for release in 1990.

Englund resides in Southern California with his wife, Nancy.

Contact: Paul Gendreau
(213) 280-2214

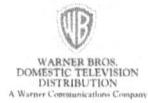

ROBERT SHAYE
(Executive Producer)

Since founding New Line Cinema in 1967, Robert Shaye has served as President and Chief Executive Officer where he has overseen the acquisition and marketing of such popular releases as "Sympathy for the Devil," "The Seduction of Mimi," the re-release of the cult hit "The Texas Chainsaw Massacre" and the 1978 Academy Award winner for Best Foreign Film, "Get Out Your Handkerchiefs." He has also served as executive producer for New Line on the feature films "Stunts," "Alone in the Dark," "The First Time," "Xtro," "Polyester," "Critters," "Quiet Cool" and the five "Nightmare on Elm Street" films. Prior to founding New Line, he produced and directed such award-winning short films as "Image" and "On Fighting Witches."

Shaye received a B.B.A. degree from the University of Michigan School of Business Administration and an L.L.B. from Columbia Law School. Selected as a Fullbright Scholar in the field of copyright law, he is currently a member of the state of New York Bar Association.

Contact: Paul Gendreau
(213) 280-2214

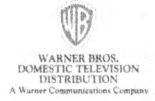

WARNER BROS.
DOMESTIC TELEVISION
DISTRIBUTION
A Warner Communications Company

SCOTT A. STONE
(Executive Producer)

With the creation of Stone Television, executive producer Scott Stone takes another step in an impressive career in television development and production.

Born in Massachusetts, Stone was raised in Indianapolis, Indiana. Pursuing an early interest in television entertainment and communications, Stone graduated with honors in 1978 from the University of Southern California Film School. In 1980 he formed Samstone Productions which produced industrials, commercials and syndicated programs including "An All Star Tribute To Jazz" starring George Benson. The following year Stone joined Telepictures Corporation as Director of Creative Services and was soon promoted to Vice President of Program Development.

The merging of Telepictures with Lorimar resulted in Stone's elevation to Senior Vice President, First-Run Television, overseeing development, programming and production including the enormously successful "The People's Court" and "Love Connection." Stone also helmed the "$1,000,000 Chance Of A Lifetime" as co-creator and executive producer.

Through Stone Television, Scott Stone continues to develop and produce quality television programming for a wide audience with such projects as the first-run late night suspense series "Freddy's Nightmares" and the children's game show "Fun House," both in their second seasons, and the new action game show, "College Mad House."

Contact: Paul Gendreau
(213) 280-2214

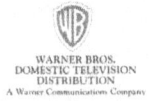

"FREDDY'S NIGHTMARES" COLOR CAPTIONS

Slide A:
Robert Englund stars as the sinister, razor-fingered Freddy Krueger
in "Freddy's Nightmares."

Slide B:
Robert Englund reprises his role as the grossly disfigured Freddy Krueger
from the blockbuster "A Nightmare on Elm Street" films in the
one-hour suspense television series "Freddy's Nightmares."

Slide C:
Robert Englund serves as host and frequent cast member Freddy Krueger
in "Freddy's Nightmares."

Slide D:
Robert Englund stars as the debonair demon of the dark, Freddy Krueger,
in "Freddy's Nightmares."

Slide E:
Robert Englund, himself.

Contact: Paul Gendreau
(213) 280-2214

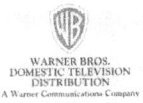

WARNER BROS.
DOMESTIC TELEVISION
DISTRIBUTION
A Warner Communications Company

Appendix I

<u>Lorimar Promotional Stills</u>

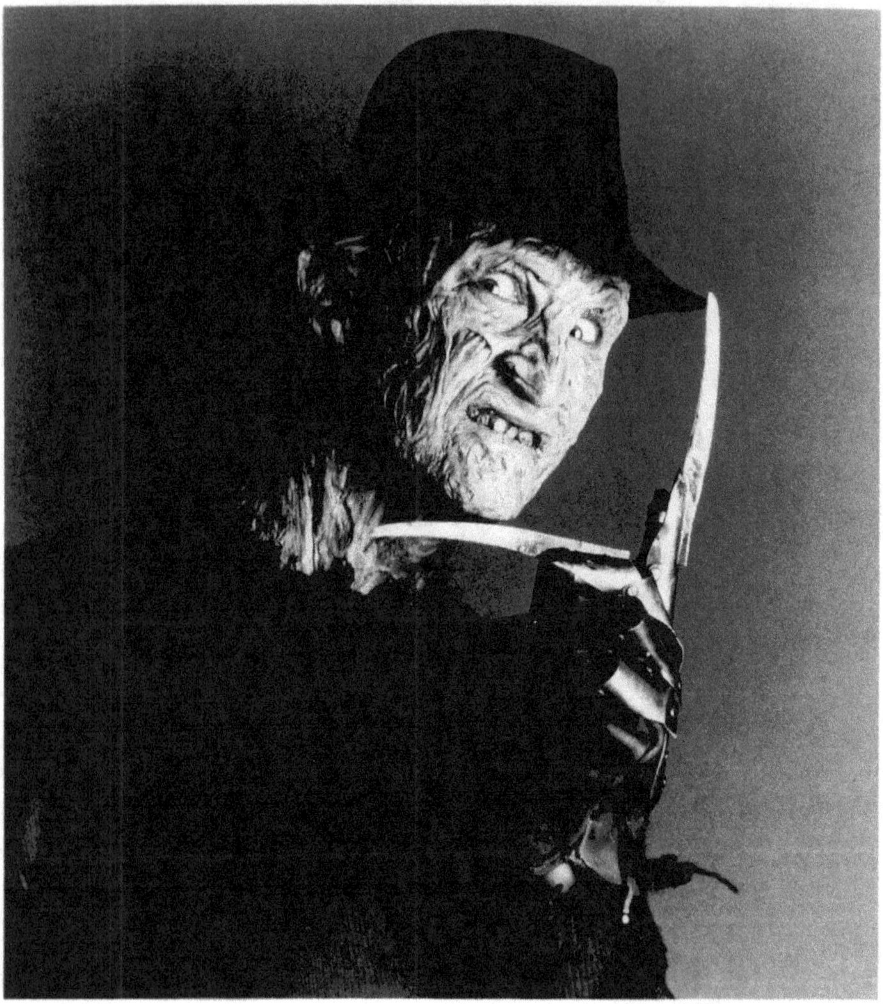

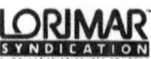
Freddy's Nightmares

A Nightmare

ON ELM STREET:
THE SERIES

ROBERT ENGLUND reprises his
role as the grossly disfigured Freddy
Krueger from the blockbuster "A
Nightmare on Elm Street" films in the
new one-hour suspense television series
"A Nightmare on Elm Street:Freddy's
Nightmares."

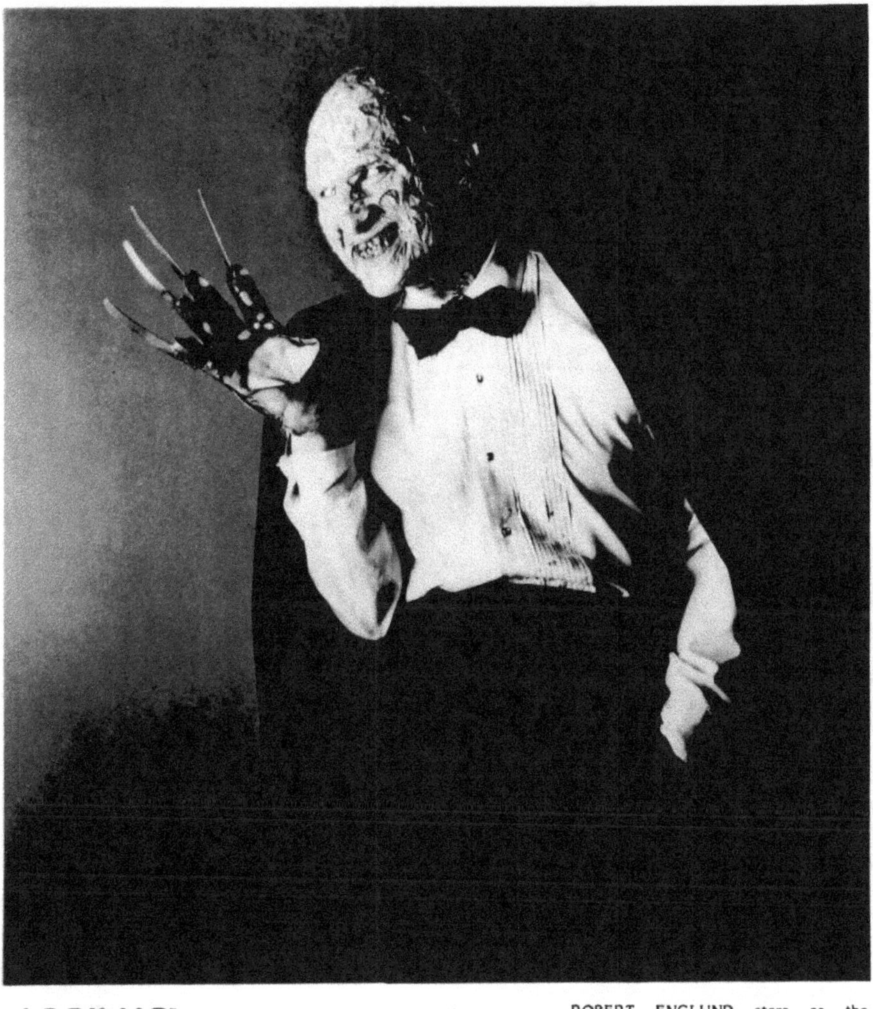

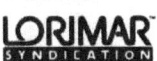

Freddy's Nightmares

A Nightmare
ON ELM STREET:
THE SERIES

ROBERT ENGLUND stars as the debonair demon of the dark, Freddy Krueger, in "A Nightmare on Elm Street:Freddy's Nightmares.

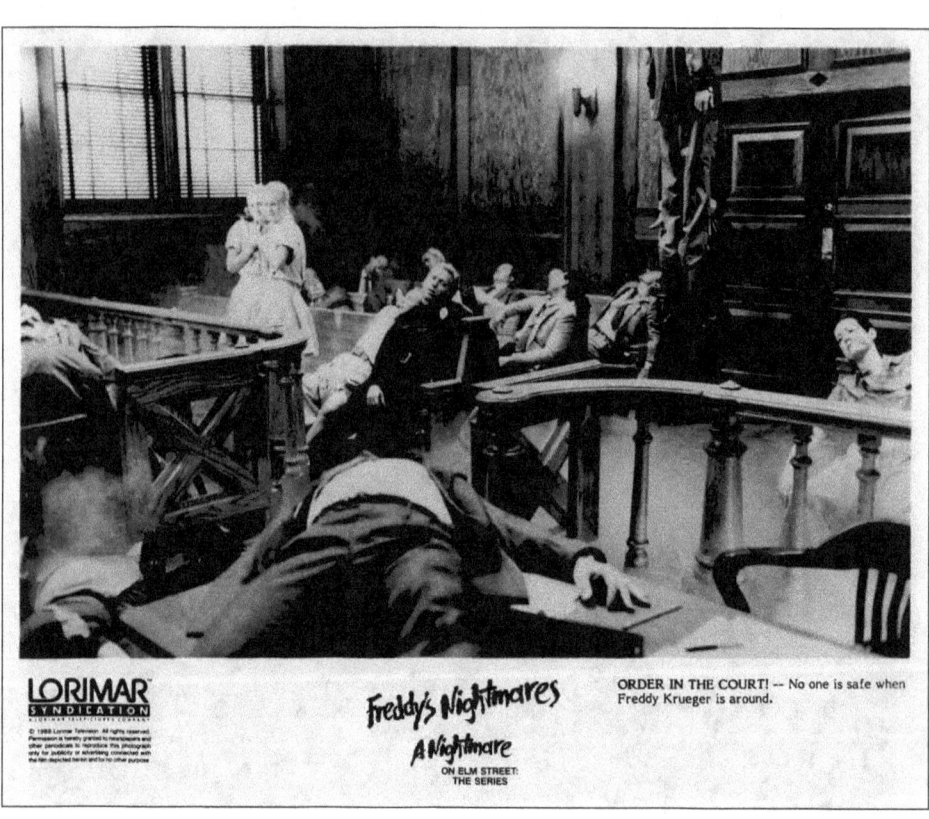

Freddy's Nightmares

A Nightmare
ON ELM STREET:
THE SERIES

ORDER IN THE COURT! -- No one is safe when
Freddy Krueger is around.

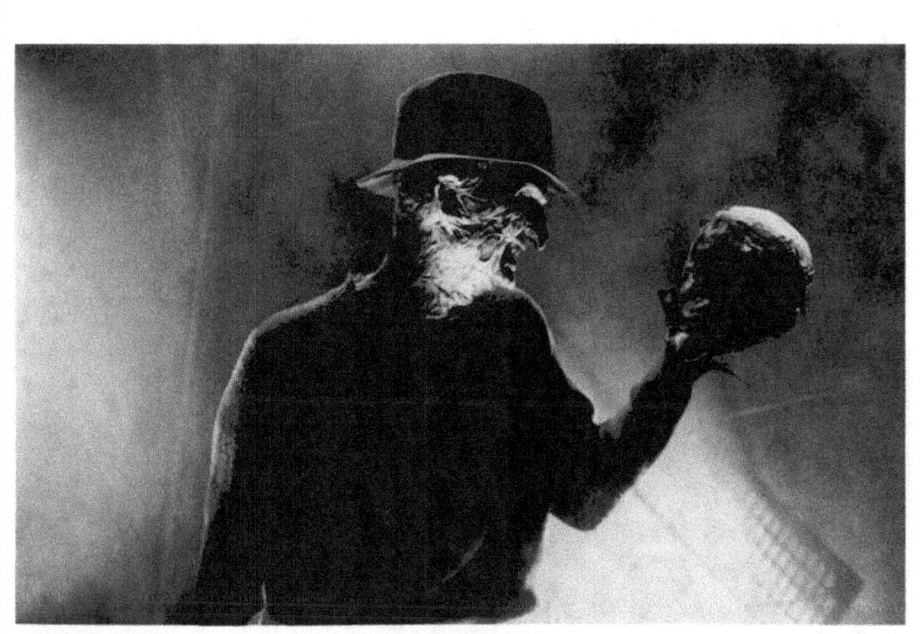

Freddy's Nightmares

A Nightmare
ON ELM STREET:
THE SERIES

A MEETING OF THE MINDS -- Freddy dissects a little
fun from a college coed who chose to experiment in
the science lab on Halloween night.

F. N. #4

143

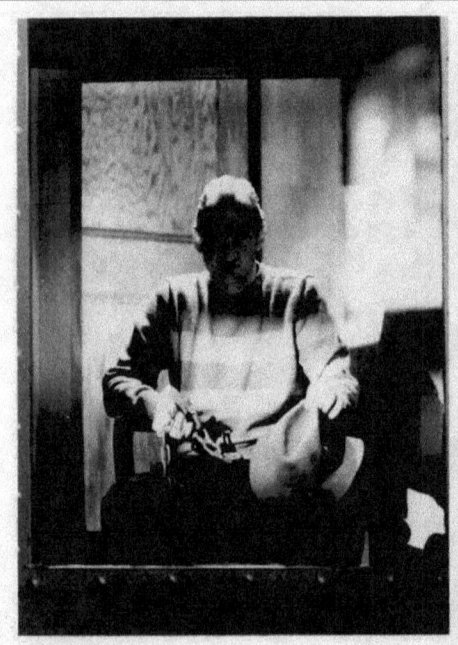 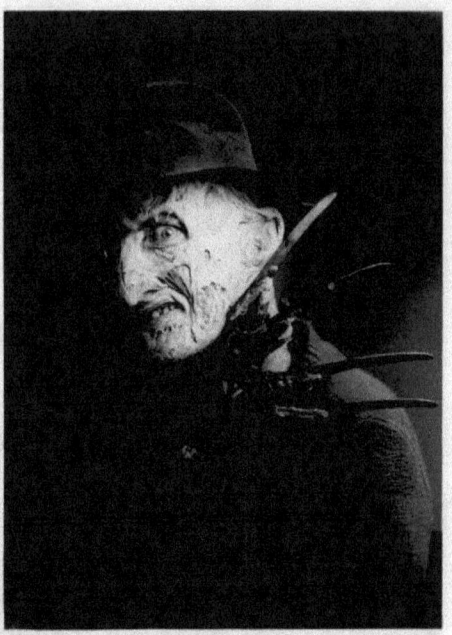

Freddy's Nightmares

A Nightmare
ON ELM STREET:
THE SERIES

FREDDY, BEFORE & AFTER -- Robert Englund stars as Freddy Krueger, the murdering maniac that was supposedly burned to death by an angry vigilante mob after he was acquitted due to a legal technicality.

BIBLIOGRAPHY

1. "New Line Television." Wikipedia, January 21, 2024.
   https://en.wikipedia.org/wiki/New_Line_Television.

2. Campbell, Richard, Bettina Fabos, and Christopher R. Martin. "Sounds and Images."
   Essay. In Media and Culture: An Introduction to Mass Communication., 224–25.
   Boston: Bedford/ St. Martin, 2014.

3. Campbell, Richard, Bettina Fabos, and Christopher R. Martin. "Sounds and Images."
   224-25.

4. "Broadcast Syndication." Wikipedia, January 2, 2024.
   https://en.wikipedia.org/wiki/Broadcast_syndication.

5. Flint, Joe. "Divine (TV) Profits." EW.com, October 17, 1997.
   https://ew.com/article/1997/10/17/divine-tv-profits/.

6. Weinberg, Rob. "Alfred Hitchcock Presents Theme: Charles Gounod." Classic FM,
   February 15, 2016.
   https://www.classicfm.com/discover-music/periods-genres/film-tv/al
   fred-hitchcock-presents-theme/.

7. "The Twilight Zone (1959 TV Series)." Wikipedia, February 15, 2024.
   https://en.wikipedia.org/wiki/The_Twilight_Zone_(1959_TV_series).

8. "Thriller (American TV Series)." Wikipedia, February 2, 2024.
   https://en.wikipedia.org/wiki/Thriller_(American_TV_series).

9. Keegan, Rebecca. The futurist: The life and films of James Cameron. New York: Three
   Rivers Press, 2010.

10. Skelton, Scott, and Jim Benson. Rod Serling's Night Gallery: An After-Hours Tour.
    Syracuse, NY: Syracuse University Press, 1999.

11. "Darkroom (TV Series)." Wikipedia, April 4, 2023.
    https://en.wikipedia.org/wiki/Darkroom_(TV_series).

12. "The Hitchhiker (TV Series)." Wikipedia, February 4, 2024.
    https://en.wikipedia.org/wiki/The_Hitchhiker_(TV_series).

13. Jr, Felix Vasquez. "'Tales from the Darkside' Brought the Anthology Frights of 'Creep
    show' to the Small Screen [TV Terrors]." Bloody Disgusting!, October 18, 2020.
    https://bloody-disgusting.com/editorials/3636680/tales-darkside-brought-
    anthology-frights-creepshow-small-screen-tv-terrors/.

14. "Amazing Stories (1985 TV Series)." Wikipedia, April 15, 2023.
    https://en.wikipedia.org/wiki/Amazing_Stories_(1985_TV_series).

15. "The Twilight Zone (1985 TV Series)." Wikipedia, February 4, 2024.
    https://en.wikipedia.org/wiki/The_Twilight_Zone_(1985_TV_series).

16. Kane, Joe. Night of the living dead: Behind the scenes of the most terrifying zombie
    movie ever., 158. New York: Citadel Press, 2010.

17. Kane, Joe. Night of the living dead: Behind the scenes of the most terrifying zombie
    movie ever., 158.

18. "New Line Cinema, Inc.." FundingUniverse, Accessed May 11, 2022.
    http://www.fundinguniverse.com/company-histories/new-line-cinema-inc-history/.

19. "ODORAMA - John Waters' Polyester." Interactive Media Archive. Accessed May 11,
    2022.
    https://interactivemediaarchive.wordpress.com/odorama-john-waters-polyester/.

20. Schwarz, Jeffrey, director. The House that Freddy Built. 2006. Automat Pictures, 2010.
    22 min. Blu-ray Disc, 1080p HD.

21. "New Line Television." Wikipedia, January 21, 2024.
    https://en.wikipedia.org/wiki/New_Line_Television.

22. Ken Wiederhorn - Columbia University in the City of New York. Accessed January 9,
    2024.
    https://www.linkedin.com/in/ken-wiederhorn-53549813.

23. "Ken Wiederhorn Interview." THE FLASHBACK FILES. Accessed January 10, 2024.
    https://www.flashbackfiles.com/ken-wiederhorn-interview.

24. "Ken Wiederhorn Interview." THE FLASHBACK FILES. Accessed January 10, 2024.
    https://www.flashbackfiles.com/ken-wiederhorn-interview.

25. Kevin Yagher productions inc.. Accessed February 16, 2024.
    https://kevinyagher.com/about/.

26. "Robert Englund Biography." Yahoo! TV. Accessed January 8, 2024.
    http://tv.yahoo.com/robert-englund/contributor/28693/bio.

27. "Everything You Ever Wanted to Know about Robert Englund." Robert Englund, Febru
    ary 6, 2021.
    https://www.robertenglund.com/about-robert/.

28. "Freddy : Dream Stalker of the Horror Flicks Turns into a Laid-Back Lagunan Who
    Likes to Surf." Los Angeles Times, March 9, 1990.
    https://www.latimes.com/archives/la-xpm-1990-03-09-li-2408-story.html.

29. "Freddy's Nightmares (a Nightmare on Elm Street: The Series) Season One Press Kit" Internet Archive. Accessed February 1, 2024. https://archive.org/details/fn-season-one_202211.

30. "Freddy's Nightmares (a Nightmare on Elm Street: The Series) Season Two Press Kit" Internet Archive. Accessed February 1, 2024. https://archive.org/details/fn-season-two.

31. "Freddy's Nightmares (A Nightmare on Elm Street: The Series) Promotional 8x10 Glossies" Internet Archive. Accessed February 1, 2024. https://archive.org/details/freddys-nightmares-promo-glossies.

ABOUT THE AUTHORS

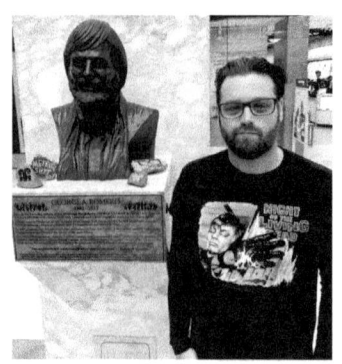

Geoff Turner is the author of *Night of the Living Tapes: The Complete Home Video History of Night of the Living Dead*, and *A Theater Near You! Advertising Night of the Living Dead*. He is an avid collector of films and film memorabilia. He can be found online sharing his collection on Instagram as @giallocaust and also running the @nightofthelivingtapes page. Geoff lives in Dayton, Ohio with his wife, Courtney, and their pets.

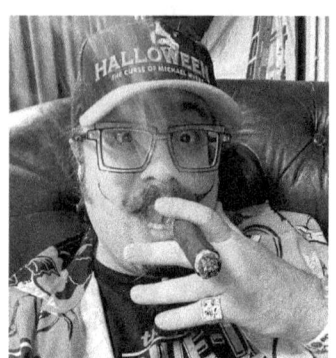

Henrique Couto is a filmmaker and podcaster from Dayton, OH. Henrique is best known for his films *Babysitter Massacre* and *Depression: The Movie*, as well as his podcasts, "Do You Even Movie?" and "Weekly Spooky." Many of his films are available on the free streaming service, Tubi. Henrique can be found online on Instagram as @henriquecouto, and through his website: www.incrediblyhandsome.com.

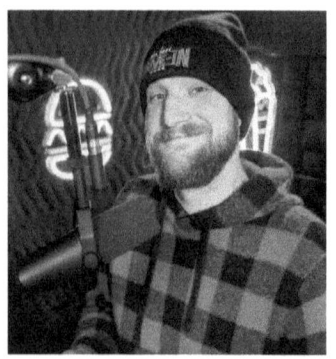

David Denoyer was born in Troy, OH, on June 6, 1992. He is a graduate of the Art Institute of Ohio in Cincinnati with an Associate's in Video Production. A life long fan of film, music, & books, he currently resides in Troy & is the Cohost of "Do You Even Movie?" Podcast with his friend Henrique. David can be found on Instagram as @davidswatchingmoviesagain.

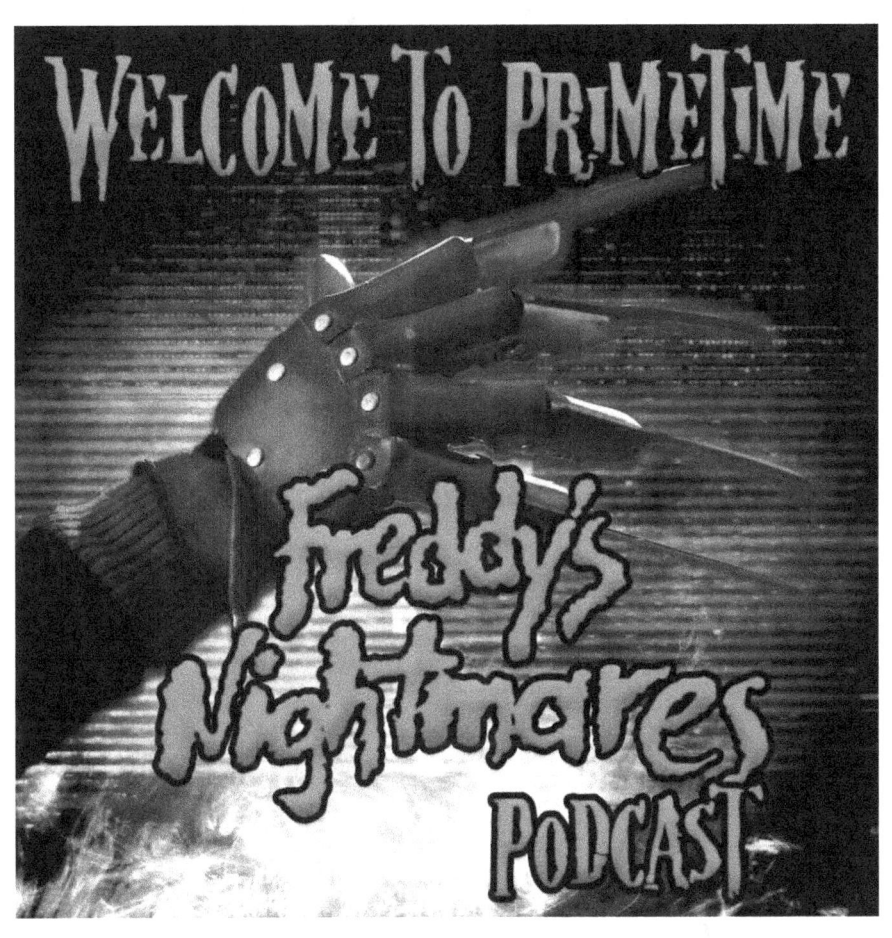

ALL EPISODES

AVAILABLE

NOW AT

WWW.FREDDYSNIGHTMARES.COM

ALSO AVAILABLE FROM

DEATH CULT PRESS

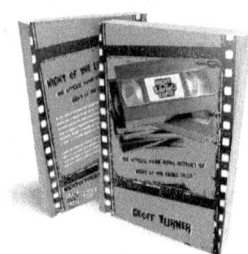
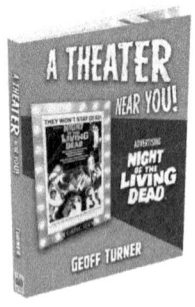

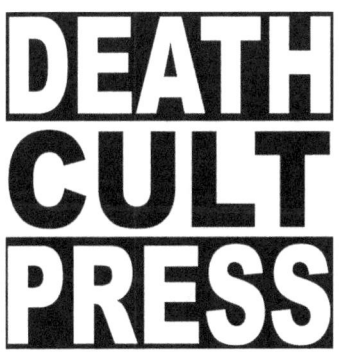